SECOND EDITION

Fed up

with the

LEGAL SYSTEM

What's Wrong & How to Fix It

formerly *Legal Breakdown:*
40 Ways to Fix Our Legal System

by Attorneys Ralph Warner &Stephen Elias

Edited by Mary Randolph & Barbara Kate Repa

NOLO PRESS BERKELEY

YOUR RESPONSIBILITY WHEN USING A SELF-HELP LAW BOOK

We've done our best to give you useful and accurate information in this book. But this book does not take the place of a lawyer licensed to practice law in your state. If you want legal advice, see a lawyer. If you use any information contained in this book, it's your personal responsibility to make sure that the facts and general information contained in it are applicable to your situation.

KEEPING UP-TO-DATE

To keep its books up-to-date, Nolo Press issues new printings and new editions periodically. New printings reflect minor legal changes and technical corrections. New editions contain major legal changes, major text additions or major reorganizations. To find out if a later printing or edition of any Nolo book is available, call Nolo Press (510-549-1976) or check the catalog in the Nolo News, our quarterly newspaper.

To stay current, follow the "Update" service in the Nolo News. You can get the paper free by sending us the registration card in the back of the book. In another effort to help you use Nolo's latest materials, we offer a 25% discount off the purchase of any new Nolo book if you turn in any earlier printing or edition. (See the "Recycle Offer" in the back of the book.) This book was last revised in: **July 1994.**

SECOND EDITION	July 1994
COVER DESIGN	Toni Ihara
BOOK DESIGN	Jackie Mancuso
PRODUCTION	Michelle Duval
PROOFREADER	Ely Newman
PRINTING	Delta Lithograph

COPYRIGHT © 1994 BY NOLO PRESS
PRINTED IN THE UNITED STATES OF AMERICA
ALL RIGHTS RESERVED

Fed up with the legal system? : what's wrong and how to fix it / by
    Nolo Press editors. -- 2nd national ed.
        p.   cm.
    Rev. ed. of: Legal breakdown. 1st ed. 1990.
    Includes index.
    ISBN 0-87337-242-5
    1. Justice, Administration of--United States. 2. Law reform-
—United States. I. Nolo Press. II. Legal breakdown.
KF384.Z9F43   1994
347.73--dc20
[347.307]   94-974
                                                         CIP

recycled paper

Acknowledgments

The writing of this book, even more than most Nolo Press projects, has been a collaborative effort. Every one of Nolo's staff of about a dozen legal writers and editors contributed. The result is an eclectic and exciting mix of ideas, woven into 42 specific proposals to reform our legal system.

We would especially like to thank Nolo editors Mary Randolph, Barbara Kate Repa and Marcia Stewart, who made substantial contributions to the second edition. Barbara Kate's expertise on healthcare issues and Marcia's extensive knowledge of consumer protection issues were crucial to the proposals on those subjects.

David Brown, Dennis Clifford, Lisa Goldoftas, Fred Horch, Catherine Jermany, Robin Leonard, Tony Mancuso, Kate McGrath and Albin Renauer also made creative contributions.

Contents

Introduction

FOR MORE THAN 20 YEARS, NOLO PRESS HAS PUBLISHED
SELF-HELP LAW BOOKS, SOFTWARE AND OTHER PRODUCTS
DESIGNED TO HELP PEOPLE FIND THEIR WAY THROUGH THE
AMERICAN LEGAL SYSTEM. OUR GOAL: TO EXPLAIN THE
PECULIAR CUSTOMS AND LANGUAGE OF LAW THOROUGHLY
AND CLEARLY, SO PEOPLE CAN HAVE DIRECT ACCESS TO IT
WITHOUT THE EXPENSIVE INTERVENTION OF A LAWYER.

This book marches to a different tune. It grew out of Nolo's
tremendous frustration with a legal system that snubs everyone
who hasn't spent three years at law school. It reflects our convic-
tion that America's laws, legal procedures and civil court system
need a total overhaul.

The barriers to every American's democratic right to a
workable system of laws makes our job a complicated one. For
example, when we explain how to look up an important consumer protection law, we also must tell people how to decipher
the almost incomprehensible jargon in which it is written.
Similarly, when we explain the mechanics of going to trial, our
discussion would be incomplete without advice on how to cope
with clerks and judges who are likely to be hostile to non-
lawyers.

Even worse is trying to explain legal procedures that would
surely have been done away with generations ago, save for the
self-interest of the legal profession. Probate—the procedure
through which a person's property is distributed after death—is
a good example. Lawyers use their potent influence in state

legislatures to keep this archaic system on the books, despite the fact that even England, the country that invented it, did away with probate in 1926. Probate is a favorite of lawyers for two reasons. First, it provides fat attorney fees when someone dies. Second, at the same time lawyers can sell people living trusts and other expensive schemes to avoid probate.

Against this background of a legal system in crisis, *Fed Up With the Legal System* sets out an agenda for legal reform and renewal. It comprises a series of practical proposals for making the American legal system more understandable, affordable and welcoming to all. Some of our ideas—such as doing away with laws that require lawyers to be involved in house sales in most states and simplifying the divorce process—would save consumers billions of dollars. Others, such as requiring laws to be written in plain English and expanding consumer-friendly small claims court, seem so obviously needed that it's mind-boggling that they weren't done years ago.

Some of the reforms we propose, such as eliminating probate, have been advanced for many years. It's fair to ask why, if they are so sensible, weren't they adopted long ago? The answer is as sad as it is simple: proposals to make our legal system more democratic have never been given a fair hearing. Instead, the legal profession has used its considerable power to consistently oppose all reforms—no matter how sensible—that threaten its monopoly over providing Americans with access to the law. The harder it is for people to solve their legal problems on their own, lawyer groups seem to reason, the more business there is for lawyers.

If you doubt this, consider for a minute your ability to solve your own legal problems. Even if you earn $25 an hour—an above-average wage—it won't be easy for you to buy services from a lawyer, given that most charge $175 to $250 per hour. You may be tempted to try to bypass lawyers and take advantage of your right to solve your own legal problems. If you do, here is what you must cope with:

☞ Laws that are hard to find and even harder to read.

☞ Unnecessary and often incomprehensible procedures that govern the most basic disputes.

☞ No forms or instructions to help you.

☞ In every court except small claims, court clerks and judges hostile to self-representation.

☞ Statutes that prescribe fines and jail for any non-lawyer (even a trained paralegal) who sells you affordable legal help.

What can we do to improve legal access? First, and most important, as citizens we can and should demand that our legislators make the dozens of changes necessary to restore to all Americans their democratic right to understand their own laws and legal procedures. *Fed Up With the Legal System* sets out many positive ways to do this. But we know from two decades of experience that trying to improve legal access from outside the system is an uphill struggle. To make these reforms happen before the end of this century, there's something else we need do: appeal to a long-lost sense of duty and responsibility of American lawyers to run an open and honest system.

An Appeal to Lawyers

Nolo was founded by lawyers who believed that the democratic promises of our legal system were not being honored. Average Americans were being priced out of civil justice by high attorney fees at the same time that the legal profession was creating more barriers to self-representation. For the most part, this process was not malicious—lawyers simply believed what they had been taught, which was that anyone who represented herself had a fool for a client.

Two decades ago it seemed hopeless to ask lawyers—most of whom didn't even realize most Americans were being shut out of the legal system—to help craft ways for people to gain direct access to the law. Nolo simply set out to create practical tools—plain English explanations of the law, forms and step-by-step instructions—that non-lawyers needed to represent themselves. To a considerable degree, this strategy has worked. Armed with self-help legal tools from Nolo and other providers, millions of consumers have acquired the power to solve their own legal problems. These modern pioneers of self-representation have done much to pry open our lawyers-only legal system. To take but one example, in many states, more than half of divorcing couples don't hire a lawyer, something that would have been impossible even ten years ago.

But despite great progress, the unfortunate truth is that even determined self-helpers can change our legal system only slowly and incrementally. Lawyers are still firmly in control of the process by which laws are made in our legislatures, carried out by legal bureaucrats and adjudicated in our courts. In short, fundamental change along the lines discussed in this book can come quickly only with the legal profession's help. So necessarily, this book is in part an appeal to the conscience of American lawyers.

We ask lawyers to do one simple thing: remember the impulse that first brought you to the law. Chances are it was at least in part the idea that by joining the legal profession you could lead an honorable life of service in the tradition of men like Lincoln, Holmes and Warren. How closely does your life as a lawyer measure up to your own early hopes? Many lawyers we know would ruefully answer "not close enough," and perhaps add that they're tired of being part of a profession that most Americans distrust and many despise.

Grappling with the question of how to lead a fulfilling life in the law, Oliver Wendell Holmes, Jr. wrote that "happiness cannot be won simply by being counsel for great corporations and having an income of fifty thousand dollars." He concluded that it was possible to "live greatly in the law," but that to do so a lawyer must look for the rational connection between the day-to-day struggle and "the frame of the universe."

We make no claim that Holmes was in favor of legal self-help, but without question he advocated that lawyers stretch their horizons beyond day-to-day concerns and interests to cope with larger questions of their profession and their lives. His advice is uncannily relevant today, when so many lawyers are hungry to find a larger purpose for their professional lives.

If lawyers would help to create a truly democratic, accessible legal system, the results could be spectacular, both for the public and the profession. Americans could solve many of their own legal problems. Some lawyers would find a fulfilling role as their helpers and coaches, while many others would be liberated from humdrum tasks to do more imaginative legal work. (And perhaps best of all, people would no longer find reason to tell all those mean lawyer jokes.)

The prospect of lawyers leading the fight to make our laws understandable, our legal procedures straightforward and our courthouses usable by all may sound like a dream. It needn't be. Many wonderful lawyers have been at the forefront of reforming many other areas of American life. From door-to-door sales, to auto safety, to honest funeral practices, to cleaning up the environment, hard-working, dedicated members of the legal profession have led the way. One of these days, this same impulse to make America a better place will be directed at our own profession. And with this renewed dedication to making the law accessible to all, lawyers will regain the public trust and respect they once commanded.

Take Simple Actions Out of Court

EACH DAY, TENS OF THOUSANDS OF "LEGAL" TASKS, INCLUDING UNCONTESTED NAME CHANGES, ADOPTIONS, DIVORCES AND PROBATES, ARE PRESENTED TO AMERICAN JUDGES. THIS IS AS NEEDLESS AS IT IS COSTLY. COURTS ARE A MISERABLE PLACE TO HANDLE ROUTINE PAPERWORK.

Courts are designed primarily to handle adversarial proceedings, where lawyers argue for each side and a great deal of time and money are spent concocting and debating legal theories. Over centuries, elaborate rules governing every nuance of courtroom procedure have evolved. As far more efficient arbitration and private court alternatives have demonstrated, precious few of these Gilbert-and-Sullivan-type formalisms are really necessary to protect people's rights, even during a full-blown trial. But for uncontested issues such as adoptions or probates, they are just plain dumb, and create an unnecessarily hostile, intimidating and expensive place to conduct business.

Some people argue that presenting uncontested actions for approval by a judge provides important protections not available in a less formal, non-judicial setting. This argument rests on the assumption that people who wear long black dresses and sit on wooden thrones are somehow more competent—or are perceived by the public to be so—than other public employees. It's doubtful.

> *In some countries, the course of the courts is so tedious, and the expense so high, that the remedy, Justice, is worse than injustice, the disease.*
>
> —BENJAMIN FRANKLIN

But even assuming there is some value to conducting some types of official business with courtly pomp, it's undeniable that most judges are busy dealing with the overwhelming number of contested matters. They seldom have the time to properly evaluate uncontested cases. No matter how you look at it, the judge's signature often adds little but ink.

Relegating uncontested matters to the courts is unnecessary and inefficient for several other reasons:

☞ Many personal decisions don't need ratification by a judge. No one gets a judge's seal of approval before marrying or having children. Similarly, the common practice of a judge formally approving a stepparent adoption—especially when a social services agency has already investigated and approved it—serves no useful purpose.

☞ Taking up court time for uncontested matters contributes mightily to the courts' increasingly huge backlog of contested cases.

☞ Courts scare people. Even though the paperwork necessary to accomplish an uncontested task may be simple (or could be made so), the fact that an appearance before a judge is involved automatically sends many people trundling off to a lawyer. The unfortunate result is that they often pay $200 an hour for a lawyer's secretary or paralegal to fill in forms that are often no more complicated than an application for a driver's license.

☞ Courts cost taxpayers a fortune to operate. An administrative procedure that eliminates the need for a paying a judge, bailiff and court clerk would save a bundle.

What to Do

Uncontested matters—adoptions, conservatorships, divorces, probates, guardianships and others—should be removed from court entirely. A few of these court procedures, such as the processes necessary to change one's name or probate an estate left to the deceased person's spouse or close family, should simply be abolished.

Other matters, such as uncontested divorces and adoptions, should be handled by administrative agencies that have the expertise to process them efficiently and knowledgeably. To protect people who should have a voice in the outcome of some types of actions (for example, close relatives of a child proposed for adoption), all those who might reasonably be expected to have an interest should be identified when the first papers are filed. In rare instances, when someone wanted to object—for example, if a grandmother wanted to challenge an adoption—the case could be transferred to a court for a full hearing.

A good system of administrative registration and regulation should have reasonable filing fees. At a minimum, all paperwork would consist of fill-in-the-blanks forms, which would be distributed with clear instructions by the agency. User-friendly computerized form preparation systems should be quickly developed. (See Proposal #17, Computerize the Law.) The agency should also provide reasonably-priced help for confused filers.

> *When the judge's mule dies, everybody goes to the funeral; when the judge himself dies, nobody goes.*
>
> —ARABIC PROVERB

How We Got Into This Mess

Nine hundred years ago, in Norman England, civil courts required plaintiff and defendant to plead their own cases. On rare occasions, granted only by royal writ, substitutes could appear. At these times, an attorney, or *responsalis*, represented the absent party. Inevitably, substitution became more and more common and soon, despite a great deal of resistance, attorneys became a fixture. These attorneys were not officers of the court or a recognized profession, but as early as the 12th century, certain names began to show up suspiciously often. By the 13th century, the idea that people with disputes had direct access to the tribunals established to resolve them was all over. Lawyers had come to dominate the courts.

The headaches started immediately. In 1240, the Abbott of Ramsey declared that none of his tenants was to bring a pleader into his courts to impede or delay justice. A revealing pronouncement of 1275 threatened imprisonment for the attorney guilty of collusive or deceitful practice. In a record of 1280, the mayor and aldermen of London lamented the ignorance and ill manners of the lawyers who practiced in the civic courts, and promised suspension for any who took money with both hands or reviled an antagonist.

Abolish Probate

THE PROBATE SYSTEM—THE COURT-SUPERVISED PROCESS
BY WHICH A DECEASED PERSON'S PROPERTY IS
DISTRIBUTED—IS IN MOST CASES A LENGTHY AND
EXPENSIVE WASTE OF TIME. AS MILLIONS OF AMERICANS
LEARN WHEN THE WILL OF A FAMILY MEMBER OR FRIEND IS
PROBATED, THE SYSTEM RARELY BENEFITS ANYONE BUT
LAWYERS.

Probate is a relic—a holdover that traces its roots to feudal
law. No other country still has a lawyer-ridden probate system
like ours. Even England, the source of our probate law, eliminated its probate court system in the 1920s.

But in this country, unless you make other arrangements
during your life, the probate court will oversee distribution of
your property after you die. The process is an elaborate, needless
legal dance, full of papers to be filed, notices to be served and
published, inventories, appraisals and court hearings. Eventually—usually, after more than a year—the court orders the
property to be turned over to the beneficiaries.

But before beneficiaries get a thing, hefty lawyer's fees are
deducted. In a typical probate, lawyer's fees consume 5%-7% of
the property—$25,000 to $35,000 of a $500,000 estate. A
recent study by the American Association of Retired Persons
estimated that American lawyers receive $1.5 billion a year in
probate fees.

Sometimes, the lawyer's fee bears no relation to the work
actually done; the lawyer charges a percentage of the value of the

> *I wasted my youth in the romantic belief that the law was a learned profession.*
>
> —Thomas Geoghegan, Attorney

estate. A number of states still have such percentage fees enshrined in statutes; unsuspecting clients are rarely told they're legally entitled to negotiate a lower fee. And even where lawyers charge for probate services by the hour, fees are often scandalously high. Most lawyers bill at upwards of $200 an hour, but turn the actual routine paperwork over to paralegals, who are paid a small fraction of that amount.

Probate's defenders are, unsurprisingly, mostly lawyers. They assert that the system protects beneficiaries by making sure they receive property left to them and protects creditors by making sure they are paid from the estate.

The reality is that very few estates need these alleged benefits. Most people use a will to leave their property to a few loved ones and to name a trusted friend or family member to supervise distribution. And most people do not have serious debt problems when they die. What debts remain can simply be paid from the property they leave. For the rare estate with tangled finances or complex legal claims, court supervision can be valuable. But that's no reason to require *all* wills to go through probate.

Because probate has become widely discredited and mistrusted, a substantial industry has grown up to show people how to avoid it. People who take the time and trouble to plan ahead can take advantage of a number of ways to leave property without having it go through probate. They can hold property in joint tenancy, put money in pay-on-death bank accounts or establish something called a living trust. With a living trust, property is usually transferred to beneficiaries within a few days or weeks after its owner's death. No court proceeding of any kind is required.

You would think the fact that living trusts and other probate avoidance devices have proved to be safe and efficient would be all the ammunition needed to do away with probate. Better think again. Lawyers, who originally reviled living trusts, have recently seized on them as a new money machine, unabashedly advertising that by using one, people can avoid "the horrors of probate." The fact that lawyers created probate and fight ferociously to keep it on the books is nowhere mentioned.

What all this amounts to is consumer fraud, plain and simple. Lawyers create and maintain the probate monster in order to sell you a system to avoid it. The Mafia, recognizing a good protection racket when they see one, must be envious.

People who go to lawyers to have a living trust drawn up may end up paying up front much of the money their heirs would have eventually shelled out for probate. Smelling profit, lawyers have rushed to provide living trusts, often charging $1,500 or more for a basic probate-avoidance trust. Fees are correspondingly higher for fancier trusts.

What to Do

A few states, including Wisconsin and Maryland, have made efforts toward simplifying probate procedures. They have streamlined procedures and encourage people to handle probate without a lawyer. California and some other states have created fill-in-the-blank forms for probate paperwork and have simplified procedures for transferring small amounts of property or property that is left to a surviving spouse.

These reforms, however, don't go nearly far enough. At the least, probate should be abolished for property left (as most is) to spouses and other close family members. But the better solution is to do away with the entire probate system, as England did way back in 1926.

People who inherit property under a will should be allowed to take legal ownership of it without court supervision. In most cases, putting inherited property into the name of the new owner is a simple process, requiring little or no paperwork—just like transferring property when you're alive. The fact that this is already done every day via half a dozen probate-avoidance schemes proves it's safe and effective.

But what if a will is contested, or other irregularities, such as trying to disinherit a spouse, are claimed? Fine. Court proceedings can and should be available. But because such challenges are quite rare, the vast majority of people would never have to face the stress and expense of a needless court proceeding.

It is revolting to have no better reason for a rule of law than that so it was laid down in the time of Henry IV.

—JUSTICE OLIVER WENDELL HOLMES, JR.

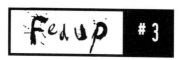

Strengthen Lemon Laws

AN ESTIMATED 100,000 OR MORE VEHICLES (AT LEAST 1% OF THE NEW CARS COMING OFF ASSEMBLY LINES EACH YEAR) ARE SERIOUSLY DEFECTIVE. BUYERS END UP TAKING THESE CARS TO AND FROM THE SHOP MONTH AFTER MONTH AFTER MONTH. LEGISLATURES HAVE TRIED TO HELP PEOPLE WHO END UP WITH THESE LEMONS, BUT TOO MANY PURCHASERS STILL END UP WITH LITTLE OR NO MEANINGFUL REDRESS.

Every state has some type of "lemon law" to protect people who buy new cars with serious problems that can't be fixed. A typical lemon law covers problems that occur within one year or the car's warranty period, whichever comes sooner. A consumer is entitled to an arbitration hearing, where a panel hears both sides of the dispute. In most states, the manufacturer must follow the panel's decision if it recommends refunding the purchase price or replacing the vehicle. A buyer who isn't satisfied with the panel's decision may be able to go to court.

Unfortunately, most lemon laws are seriously flawed. Even though arbitration hearings are often free and designed to take place without a lawyer, car manufacturers are at a distinct advantage—obviously, they are more experienced at arbitration procedures than the typical consumer. And a few auto companies establish and administer their own arbitration panels, which tend to be pro-manufacturer. In addition, some panels base their decisions only on written submissions from each side—which

> *It will be of little avail to the people that the laws are made by men of their own choice if the laws be so voluminous that they cannot be read, or so incoherent that they cannot be under-stood.*
>
> —ALEXANDER HAMILTON

doesn't allow the car owner to respond to the manufacturer's side of the story.

Second, the process takes too long. Dealers usually get three or four attempts to fix a particular defect (or approxi-mately 30 days in the shop) before a buyer can pursue lemon law remedies. After the arbitration hearing, which requires considerable preparation time, up to 60 days may elapse before a decision is made. And then more time will pass if the car buyer doesn't like the ruling and chooses to continue the fight in court.

Third, the laws are vague and too limited. The typical legal definition of a lemon is car with a "substantial defect which impairs the car's use, value or safety." Many defects don't qualify. With rare exceptions, used cars are not covered by lemon laws at all, and only half the states cover leased cars.

Fourth, the consumer unfairly bears the burden of proving that a car is a lemon. For example, the buyer may need to show that the car's market value is severely reduced because of a defect. The consumer must also show that he or she jumped through all the hoops required to get a refund or replacement. If a hoop was missed—such as failing to notify the manufacturer in writing of the defect—the case may be out the window.

Fifth, many car buyers' costs—including "consequential" damages such as renting a car while the lemon was in the shop—are not paid even if the buyer wins in arbitration. And if the buyer loses, in some states he or she must pay the cost of arbitration.

What to Do

Lemon laws could easily be improved if states would:

☞ Develop better, clearer criteria for what constitutes a lemon. The approach in Massachusetts, where a car is legally a lemon if it's in the shop for 15 business days for either one major problem or a combination of less serious defects, should be adopted nationwide.

☞ Require dealers to tell prospective buyers what percentage of the model they're considering have turned out to be lemons.

☞ Let consumers with lemons go straight to arbitration programs run by the state or by an independent consumer agency, as in New York, rather than first submitting to a manufacturer's program.

☞ Allow oral arbitration hearings, and give the car buyer the right to receive a copy of all papers the manufacturer presents so there are no surprises at the hearing.

☞ Require panels to decide cases within 40 days and allow them to reimburse consumers for consequential damages.

☞ Expand lemon law coverage to leased cars.

☞ Expand coverage to used cars, at least for major systems such as brakes, power train and engine.

☞ Produce brochures on lemon laws and consumer rights for dealers to give new car buyers at the time of purchase. These booklets should explain what consumers need to document their case before arbitration and include a step-by-step guide to the arbitration process.

Resources

Lemon Book (Ralph Nader, Clarence Ditlow and Center for Auto Safety, 1990). An excellent book on buying and owning a new car, including how to avoid buying a lemon, legal rights and remedies, and state-by-state lemon laws.

To find out about your state's lemon law and how to use it, contact your state's Attorney General's office or consumer protection agency.

For information on safety problems with your car's make and model, contact:

National Highway Traffic Safety Administration
Auto Safety Hotline
400 7th Street, SW
Washington DC 20590
(800) 424-9393

Center for Auto Safety
2001 S Street, NW
Washington DC 20009
(202) 328-7700

A buyer needs 100 eyes, a seller not one.

—GEORGE HERBERT
ENGLISH POET

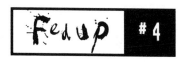

Simplify Legal Paperwork

COURTS REQUIRE DOCUMENTS TO BE WRITTEN NEW FOR EACH LEGAL PROCEDURE, LAID OUT ACCORDING TO ARBITRARY RULES AND TYPED ON A KIND OF NUMBERED PAPER USED NOWHERE ELSE. THIS COMPLEXITY BOTH INTIMIDATES PEOPLE WHO GO TO COURT WITHOUT A LAWYER AND WASTES THE TIME OF LAWYERS AND COURTS.

Drafting legal documents has been a lucrative skill among lawyers for centuries. From the start, American courts were saddled with a cumbersome array of documents. Their models were the English courts of the time, which even then were notorious for requiring intricate documents written in Latin.

Trumped-up complexity, of course, has always been the lifeblood of lawyers. Mastering the elaborate paperwork of the legal system is one of their most salable skills. Anyone who wants access to the courts must hire a lawyer who knows how to draw up papers that will open the courtroom door.

Not until very recently—within the last 20 years—did a few courts abandon the idea of documents crafted for each situation. These courts realized that they could simplify their own work considerably by using standardized, fill-in-the-blanks forms. Lawyers who completed well-designed forms were more likely to supply the data the court needed than those who prepared old-style pleadings.

Even lawyers who at first resisted quickly found standardized forms to be a bonanza. Forms made many of their tasks much simpler—and so easier to delegate to secretaries and paralegals.

> *...A piece of paper, blown by the wind into a law court may in the end only be drawn out again by two oxen.*
>
> —CHINESE PROVERB

One unintended consequence of easy-to-use forms is a huge increase in the number of people who handle their own legal problems. It's no coincidence that California, which pioneered the use of standardized forms, leads the country in court cases filed without lawyers.

A couple who wants to get an uncontested divorce, for example, wouldn't know how to write a legal request for one. But they can fill out a simple form that asks questions about their income, property and children. It is comparable to the difference between filling out an income tax return and writing a narrative to explain your income, deductions and tax due. Of course, the IRS, which is designed to get quick results, has had forms for generations.

Standardized paperwork also encourages people to be less dependent on lawyers and instead get help from self-help materials and legal typing services. Someone who doesn't want to go it alone can use a self-help book that contains tear-out forms and instructions. Or, for more help, a typing service staffed by non-lawyers—often, former legal secretaries or paralegals—will know how to prepare and file the forms correctly.

Unfortunately, standardized forms are still the rare exception to the rule. Few courts offer them, and in most places they are available only for a few matters, such as temporary restraining orders. And even courts that have forms pass them out without instructions, leaving people to fend for themselves.

What to Do

Standardized forms should be available for most routine legal matters: requesting or opposing eviction, adoption, child support, filing a personal injury lawsuit, probate and divorce are obvious ones.

All standardized forms should come with clear, line-by-line instructions. This is a truly radical notion in a system based on hiding the smallest instruction. It shouldn't be. Comprehensive instructions on how, where and when to file legal documents would not only make the task easier for those who file, it would free up court personnel to deal more efficiently with the business of the courts. People should also be able to get help from court clerks, over the phone and in person.

Computer technology offers a potential bonanza when it comes to producing legal forms. Easy-to-use computers can be installed in courthouses and other public places, so people can follow step-by-step instructions to print out the legal forms they need. (See Proposal #17, Computerize the Law.)

In indenture or deed
Tho' a thousand you read
Neither comma nor colon
you'll ken;
A stop intervening,
Might determine the meaning
And what would the lawyers do then?

—SAMUEL BISHOP

Where Things Went Wrong

Efforts at simplifying legal paperwork and procedure have proceeded in fits and starts for the entire history of this country. The colonists allowed the use of English instead of Latin, for example, but complexities soon crept in. Before 1700, lawyers—who had originally been barred in many colonies—had already imported writs of *scire facias*, lawsuits for *trespass de bonis asportatis* and other similarly mysterious creatures. Judges took on kingly airs, throwing out cases if the papers misspelled a name, gave the defendant's occupation incorrectly or made other trivial errors.

As the legal profession grew in power during the 18th and early 19th centuries, the relatively simple colonial procedures were gradually submerged under a tide of complexity. For their inspiration, lawyers looked back (some would say backwards) to the intricate English system of pleading.

In the mid-1800s, the pendulum swung back in a more democratic direction. People no longer needed law licenses to appear in court in many states, and there were a number of efforts to make law more understandable. The most revolutionary breakthrough in procedure came when a New York commission proposed a radically simplified system of pleading. The idea was to make the paperwork straightforward enough so that the average person could go to court without a lawyer. Many lawyers, of course—the same folks who brought us *trespass de bonis asportatis*—fought the idea. But it caught on, especially in the newer western states.

Further reform efforts have been stalled for most of this century. Bar associations consolidated their hold on the legal system, and there have been few crusaders to attack the red tape of the courts. But as public outrage again grows at a system that needlessly freezes out all but lawyers, that may change.

Make the Courthouse User-Friendly

PEOPLE HAVE THE RIGHT TO REPRESENT THEMSELVES IN
COURT WITHOUT A LAWYER. BUT IF THEY TRY, THEY
OFTEN FIND THAT COURTHOUSES ARE SET UP BY AND FOR
LEGAL PROFESSIONALS AND ARE NEEDLESSLY HARD FOR
EVERYONE ELSE TO NAVIGATE.

It's obvious, from the moment you walk in, that lawyers see
courthouses as their private clubs. Unlike most government
facilities, there's rarely a central information desk or window.
The kind of informative pamphlets typically found in a Social
Security, motor vehicle registration or IRS office are also absent.
Often there are special lounges, work areas and phones for
lawyers, but benches and pay phones for everyone else.

Court clerks' offices, where every significant paper must be
filed, are confusing and intimidating. Trying to do business
there can seem like a bad dream in which you are lost and need
help, only to be faced with perpetually hurrying people, un-
marked information windows and long lines of people who don't
speak your language. Nowhere will you find a simple sign that
says "Non-Lawyer Information" or "Non-Lawyers File Papers
Here."

Assuming you get your papers filed and your hearing day
arrives, even finding the right courtroom can be exhausting. In
many courthouses, hundreds of litigants and lawyers must crowd

There is no reason why a plain, honest man should not be permitted to go into court and tell his story and have the judge before whom he comes permitted to do justice in that particular case, unhampered by a great variety of statutory rules... We have got our procedure regulated according to the trained, refined, subtle, ingenious intellect of the best practiced lawyers, and it is all wrong.

—ELIHU ROOT, 1845-1937
U.S. SECRETARY OF STATE

into a single room every morning while a judge or clerk reads off courtroom assignments in semi-code, with the speed of a tobacco auctioneer. For example, "*Smith v. Evans* to 17, trailing," means that case will eventually be heard in Courtroom 17, after some other cases go first. Which raises another big problem for non-lawyers: Lawyers can often take advantage of the fact that lots of hearings are scheduled for the same time by scurrying from one courtroom to another, but people who represent themselves must cool their heels—sometimes for days.

Lack of respect for the public is also reflected in courtroom procedures. People without lawyers often don't know exactly where to sit or stand, or how to approach or address the judge. A simple pamphlet with a clear instructions on how to accomplish these most basic of tasks would be quick and easy to put together. It has never been done.

Most court clerks, lawyers and judges, for whom the current system is familiar and comfortable, don't even see the many barriers that deny non-lawyers equal access to the legal system. They have been trained to believe that to enter the judicial system, citizens really should pay a gatekeeper—a lawyer.

What to Do

Courts must be examined from top to bottom with an eye to eliminating this pervasive and essentially anti-democratic bias. Here are just a few of the things courts need to do:

☞ Publish an "access catalog," designed like a college course catalog, that describes what the court can do for people. It should spell out how much a procedure costs, how long it takes and where to find more information.

☞ Like other complicated bureaucracies, every courthouse should have employees—advisors and filing clerks—whose only job is to help people navigate the courts. They could be paid for by filing fees paid by non-lawyers.

☞ Courts should distribute instructional materials to help people with routine court procedures. For example, printed forms for a simple divorce, stepparent adoption or guardianship should be available, with complete instructions. The answers to frequently asked questions should be available in pamphlets, books, computer databases and recorded telephone messages. Videotapes that show how the courtroom process works should be readily available at the courthouse.

☞ Courthouses should take a look at their designs, with an eye to making them usable by ordinary citizens. Start with simple aids such as clear signs and information booths, and move toward providing other services such as work stations, evening court sessions and drop-in childcare for parents who must go to court.

☞ To ensure accountability, a non-lawyer board of directors could monitor a courthouse's treatment of the public. Such a board could also deal with complaints from the public.

Resources

Two recent studies by the ABA Standing Committee on the Delivery of Legal Services show how courts can better accommodate people doing their own law work.

Self Representation in Divorce Cases explores how the Maricopa County, Arizona courts are dealing with the flood of people doing their own divorces. Among other innovations, the courts are experimenting with computerized kiosks that produce divorce forms and eviction notices, in English and Spanish.

Responding to the Needs of the Self-Represented Divorce Litigant explores experiments by a number of courts designed to make it easier for people to handle their own divorces.

Vision 2020, a study by a special California commission, recommended an overhaul of California courts to better accommodate all litigants, whether or not they are represented by a lawyer.

> *Poor people have access to the courts in the same sense that the Christians had access to the lions when they were dragged into a Roman arena.*
>
> —JUDGE EARL JOHNSON, JR.

Mediate Child Custody and Support Disputes

FEW EVENTS IN MODERN LIFE PRODUCE MORE BITTERNESS AND HURT THAN CHILD CUSTODY DISPUTES, ESPECIALLY WHEN CHILDREN ARE YOUNG. SADLY, THE AMERICAN LEGAL SYSTEM DOES MUCH TO MAKE THESE DISAGREEMENTS MORE MISERABLE. ADVERSARIAL COURT PROCEDURES FAN PARANOIA, ENCOURAGE PERJURY AND TURN CHILDREN INTO EXPENDABLE PAWNS IN AN EMOTIONAL BATTLE.

Our legal system magnifies disputes over child custody, visitation and support by encouraging parents to fight them out in the hostile arena of a courtroom. Sometimes these battles last for years, or until money to pay the lawyers runs out, with each parent escalating the attack to meet or beat the other.

Fortunately, there is a better approach: mediation. Styles of mediation vary somewhat, but the main idea is that those faced with a dispute meet with a neutral third person and attempt to work out their own settlement. Unlike a court or arbitration proceeding, however, no decision is imposed on those who have the dispute. It's up to them to keep talking until they arrive at a compromise.

The mediator's role is to see that each person gets a fair chance to speak, ensure that neither is intimidated or overbearing and perhaps to make suggestions to help the parties reach an agreement. Where state law sets guidelines for child support

> *Divorce involves not only facts but feelings, and we're not able to legislate feelings.*
>
> —ANN L. MILNE,
> DIVORCE MEDIATOR

based on parental income, the mediator must also see that the agreement complies. In addition, most mediators reserve the right to veto any custody or support agreement that's clearly not in the long-term best interests of the children.

Despite the advantages of mediation, most people take custody disputes to court. Lawyers and judges trained to resolve disputes in an adversarial manner rarely voluntarily refer people to mediation. Private mediation programs run by psychologists, social workers, clergy or lawyers-turned-mediators have kept many people out of court. But private mediators typically charge from $75 to $200 per hour—out of reach for many people.

Mandatory court-sponsored programs that provide free mediation have been more successful in helping people who have disputes over child custody or support. The laws in 11 states require that people try free public mediation before fighting out their differences in court. An additional 20 states authorize their judges to order it. The success rate of mandatory mediation programs has been impressive: a success rate in the 80% range is common.

Mediation is vastly superior to a court fight. But like any human system, it's not perfect. First, to make intelligent decisions, each spouse needs good, detailed information about state laws on custody, support and visitation. Most mediators don't provide it.

Second, mediation raises the risk that a spouse with more business sense or psychological power will be able to coerce the other into agreeing to an inequitable result. One parent may accept an inadequate amount of child support or allow the other parent to unfairly dominate child-rearing decisions.

Third, if mediation is voluntary, a parent may pretend to mediate in good faith while following the instructions of a lawyer to let the mediation fail so the dispute can be taken into trial court.

What to Do

At the outset, separating parents should be given a thorough and easy-to-understand pamphlet explaining their legal rights and responsibilities toward their children. This should cover custody, visitation and support requirements.

All courts that handle divorce and custody disputes should have a free mediation program. Both married and unmarried couples who have disputes over children should be required to use this program, or a private mediator, before taking a contested custody or visitation dispute to court. If a mediating couple agrees on child support, custody and visitation, their agreement falls within state guidelines, and the mediator certifies that it is uncoerced and in the best interests of the children, it should take effect at once. If parents cannot agree after a reasonable number of mediation sessions, the dispute should be referred to court, along with the mediator's recommendation.

What's the difference between a tick and a lawyer?

The tick drops off when you're dead.

Regulate Contingency Fees

WHEN HANDLING CAR ACCIDENT AND OTHER CIVIL CASES THAT PROMISE BIG DOLLARS, LAWYERS OFTEN TAKE A LARGE PERCENTAGE OF THE AMOUNT RECOVERED AS THEIR FEES. TYPICALLY, THESE FEES FAR EXCEED A REASONABLE RATE FOR THE SERVICES RENDERED OR THE RISK TAKEN. AS A RESULT, BILLIONS OF DOLLARS ARE DIVERTED FROM CLIENTS DIRECTLY INTO LAWYERS' BANK ACCOUNTS.

In lawsuits over personal injuries, lawyers customarily charge a "contingency fee" of 25% to 50% of the award or settlement. This means the lawyer gets paid very generously if the case is won, and nothing if it's lost.

In theory, this approach makes some sense. An injured person can get a lawyer's services without paying for them unless there is a successful result. Many people who can't afford to pay a lawyer's hourly rates can have their cases presented in court.

On closer examination, however, the contingency fee system amounts to little more than a get-rich-quick scheme for lawyers. Lawyers who win or favorably settle a contingency fee case almost always get paid far more than the time spent on the case justifies. Many personal injury attorneys earn hundreds of times more with contingency fees than they would if they charged by the hour.

For example, take the case of 21 children killed in a school bus accident. The bus had been hit by a soft-drink delivery truck, and the beverage company's insurance company quickly agreed to pay $122 million. According to Professor Lester

> *I seek the kind of verdict that makes the angels sing and the cash registers ring.*
>
> —MELVIN BELLI,
> PERSONAL INJURY LAWYER

Brickman, of the Benjamin Cardozo Law School, the lawyers who represented the children's families received the equivalent of $25,000 an hour for their services.

Proof that contingency fee cases are outrageously profitable is found in a common practice of personal injury lawyers: They hand over one-third of the contingency fee to the lawyer who referred the case to them.

Personal injury lawyers justify these windfalls by arguing that they need large fees to balance out the cases where there is no recovery and they aren't paid for their work. But this argument is based on the false premise that when they take a case for no up-front fee, they also take a substantial risk of coming up empty-handed. The examples most often cited are complex, expensive lawsuits against big corporations that poison the environment or their employees. But these cases are the exceptions. Most lawyers accept cases only if:

☞ a favorable outcome is reasonably certain based on the facts and the law;

☞ the damages suffered by the client will generate enough fees to make taking the case well worth the lawyer's while; and

☞ one of the defendants is an insurance company, city, corporation or other "deep pocket," which can afford either to buy its way out of the case by settling or pay a judgment if the case goes to trial.

The harm this scam causes to society is enormous. In addition to the billions of dollars siphoned off from injured victims, the possibility of huge contingency fee profits creates a kind of

lawyer feeding frenzy. Not a few lawyers bring lawsuits on flimsy grounds or concoct massive class actions—lawsuits in which a small group of individuals sue on behalf of a large group of similarly affected people—seeking hundreds of millions of dollars in damages. Some even assist clients in presenting perjured testimony. All of these lawsuits in turn contribute to horrendous insurance rates for everyone.

What to Do

To correct contingency fee abuse, some kinds of lawsuits—for example, auto accident and medical malpractice cases—should be handled administratively on a no-fault basis. A lawyer should not be necessary, except perhaps to give limited legal advice or to help handle an appeal if an administrative claim is denied.

When a lawyer is necessary, a client who doesn't want to pay an hourly rate could still agree to a contingency fee. Such fees could be useful and fair—but not if they are based only on the amount won. Instead, the fee could be based on the amount of work done, but also give the winning lawyer a bonus for taking a truly risky case on a contingency basis.

At the start of the case, the lawyer should be required to give the client a detailed, written estimate of the basic fee. That estimate would be based on the anticipated number of hours the case would require from lawyers, paralegals and clerical staff. It would also include a ceiling on the fee if the hourly estimate proved inadequate.

To assess the chances of winning the case, the estimate would spell out:

☞ how clear the defendant's liability is;

☞ how difficult it will be to prove the extent of the injury; and

☞ how likely it is that the defendant will pay a settlement or judgment.

In addition, the lawyer and client could agree on a bonus—perhaps a small percentage of the amount won. But the client wouldn't have to fork over a third or more of the award, as is the case under the current system.

To keep lawyers honest, if the case is won or successfully settled, the lawyer would have to submit to the trial court the fee agreement and documentation of hours worked. This material would be part of the case file, accessible to the public.

If the case is lost, the lawyer would not get paid unless the risk in the case had been assessed to be over 50%, and the client agreed in writing, on the basis of the risk assessment, to be responsible for the fees regardless of the outcome. The lawyer's initial assessment could be reviewed by a fee arbitration panel at the client's request.

If the judge deemed the lawsuit to be in the public interest—a case against a toxic polluter or manufacturer of unsafe cars, for example—the judge would still have authority to decide whether attorneys should be paid by the defendant.

> *What's the difference between terrorists and lawyers?*
>
> *Terrorists have sympathizers.*

Living the Good Life With Contingency Fees

An advertisement in *The Recorder*, a San Francisco legal newspaper, sported the headline "Millionaire Personal Injury Attorney Reveals Secrets." The ad touted a three-day seminar, generously promising to show other personal injury lawyers how to "unlock the door to incredible wealth in the personal injury field." The ad proclaimed that any lawyer can "handle 50-60 cases simultaneously, settle most cases within 60-90 days, [and] consistently get the highest settlements," all without increasing overhead.

The price? A flat $30,000. Anticipating that some might balk at this price, the ad offered a money-back guarantee. But given what attorneys can get under the contingency fee system if it is milked properly, $30,000 for a seminar is probably a small price to pay.

Add Self-Help Court Clerks

CLERKS ARE THE GATEKEEPERS OF THE COURTHOUSE.
NO LEGAL ACTION IS POSSIBLE UNTIL THEY PUT THEIR
STAMPS OF APPROVAL ON PAPERS FILED WITH THE COURT.
UNFORTUNATELY, MANY CLERKS ARE INDIFFERENT,
HOSTILE OR JUST TOO BUSY TO HELP PEOPLE WHO TRY TO
NAVIGATE THE COURT SYSTEM WITHOUT LAWYERS.

Most court clerks refuse to answer simple procedural questions from people who need to file routine legal paperwork. Left on their own—without help, standardized forms or even rudimentary instructions—many people submit papers that these same clerks then reject for trivial errors. To add insult to injury, clerks commonly refuse to explain why papers are inadequate or to direct self-helpers to materials that could give them guidance. Because many self-helpers cannot afford to hire a lawyer for assistance, they are shut out of the legal system.

Clerks are under pressure from their supervisors—judges and court administrators—to deal quickly with people waiting in line. And they often defend their actions by arguing that assisting self-helpers is too time-consuming. They are partially right. It *is* time-consuming to help people who are unfamiliar with the legal labyrinth. But it's time well spent. Guaranteeing all people access to the legal system should be treated as a priority, not an irksome chore.

Clerks also protest that requiring them to give self-helpers too much direction would put them at risk of being sued for giving faulty advice or prosecuted for practicing law without a

> *A long habit of not thinking a thing wrong gives it a superficial appearance of being right, and raises at first a formidable outcry in defense of custom.*
>
> —THOMAS PAINE

license, a criminal offense. So they hide behind a familiar refrain: We Are Not Authorized To Give Legal Advice. Their fear, however, is ungrounded. There are no reported cases of court clerks who have been prosecuted for the unauthorized practice of law.

What to Do

In every court, clerks should be trained and directed to help everyone—not just those with law licenses—who seeks access to the courts.

To alleviate court clerks' fear of legal prosecution, statutes prohibiting the unauthorized practice of law and punishing malpractice could easily be rewritten to exempt clerks who dispense basic information to the public. The new statutory definitions would sensibly include the prosaic motions of handing out legal forms and giving cursory instructions for filling in the blanks on them.

Certain clerks should be designated to provide assistance, in person and on the phone, to people who are handling a legal matter without a lawyer. The self-help clerks would be experts in court procedures and specially trained in dealing with the problems and pitfalls of legal paperwork. For example, they could tell a divorcing couple what forms they need to fill out for a simple, uncontested divorce, and could answer basic questions about how to fill them out. Ideally, the clerks could also distribute the required forms, along with line-by-line instructions on how to complete them.

Self-help clerks would not advise people about the law or help with the strategy for a lawsuit. If someone really needed legal advice, the clerks could recommend self-help materials or recommend getting an experienced lawyer's advice.

Because helping self-helpers through the system would be their sole task, the self-help clerks would not suffer the hurry-up angst that afflicts most other courtroom personnel. When they took the time needed to explain a convoluted procedure, they would simply be doing their job—not slowing down the line for those who waited behind.

A good model for such a program is the system of small claims court legal advisors used in California. These advisors are available to help people who want to sue or are being sued in small claims court. They answer questions about filing procedures, preparing and presenting cases, and collecting judgments after cases have been decided.

The additional clerks' salaries could come from some of the document filing fees, which in many places are currently earmarked for such items as coffee and other niceties for judges and lawyers. If that didn't cover all the expense, people who needed assistance from self-help clerks could pay for it with slightly higher filing fees.

Any time a lawyer is seen but not heard, it's a shame to wake him.

A Different Approach in Wisconsin: Court Clerks Who Help Self-Helpers

In Madison, Wisconsin, those filing for probate after the death of a family member or friend have two choices. They can pay an attorney to do the job for them. Or they can handle it themselves in a specialized informal probate procedure that is part of the county court system. Those who go it alone have lots of help: forms, instructions and explanations from Probate Court Commissioner Daniel Breunig and his staff of three. They meet with those who file informally to discuss the probate process generally and go over a checklist of forms that must be prepared and filed.

The forms are straightforward. To complete them, people need only fill in information such as names and addresses. Breunig says what people need the most is assurance that they have filled in the blanks properly.

When the simplified system went into effect in 1973, some predicted that as many as 90% of all probates filed in Wisconsin would be processed through the informal system. That never came to pass. Breunig says that only about one-third of the approximately 1,200 probates filed annually in Wisconsin are handled without lawyers.

Breunig says there are two reasons for this. "Traditionally, most people have believed the attorneys who have always told them, 'I'm this Superhero and I can do something you can't do,'" says Breunig. Another group of people, he says, would rather hire someone else to do their legwork and paperwork.

Those who file informally get almost unlimited help from Breunig and his staff along the way. "In two or three hours, we can steer someone through a conventional probate," Breunig says. "They save about $4,000 in attorneys' fees. But what they accomplish is even more amazing: They've conquered the grand mystique of the law."

Educate the Public About Law

OUR SCHOOLS GIVE STUDENTS NEXT TO NO BASIC LEGAL TRAINING. MOST PEOPLE LEARN ABOUT LAW ONLY WHEN FACED WITH A CRISIS SUCH AS A CUSTODY BATTLE OR DISPUTE WITH A LANDLORD. BY THEN, IT'S OFTEN TOO LATE TO GATHER ENOUGH INFORMATION SHORT OF BUYING IT FROM A LAWYER.

Everyone agrees that law governs more and more aspects of our lives. Schools, especially, pay lofty lip service to the importance of an informed citizenry. Yet absurdly, the schools never teach the basic legal concepts that will inevitably affect their students' lives within a few years—the laws that control marriage, divorce, renting an apartment, getting a job or buying a house.

Things get no better after students graduate. In most communities, there is no easy access to practical legal information. The few adult programs that do exist are typically administered, catch-as-catch-can, by bar associations, whose financial self-interest is to enhance the status of attorneys as the source of all legal information. An example is the annual Law Day, May 1. Typically, lawyers make appearances on local television or at public meetings and answer legal questions. Often, the answer ends with a recommendation that the questioner hire a lawyer. Other legal education programs, including workshops or bro-

> *What do you get when you cross the Godfather with a lawyer?*
>
> *An offer you can't understand.*

chures produced by well-meaning consumer protection agencies, tend to be incomplete, irregular, publicized poorly and not widely distributed.

What to Do

Public legal education programs—beginning in the primary school classroom and continuing through adulthood—should be expanded. Educators, not practicing lawyers, need to be in charge. Most lawyers are so predisposed to seeing the law as their own property that it's impossible for them to grasp that legal information—like physics, beekeeping or Greek mythology—can be efficiently and widely taught.

States should require and fund law-related education as an ongoing part of the public school curriculum, particularly in high schools. To accomplish this, teachers need materials and training on how to make everyday law come alive. It shouldn't be hard—students are curious about how all sorts of laws affect them and their families. Laws involving curfews, reproductive rights, even the right of school officials to search their lockers are just a few good examples.

A step in the right direction can be found in the "street law" programs now sponsored by law schools throughout the country. In these programs, law students are trained and given classroom materials; they then teach high school classes about practical legal problems, including housing and family law and how to resolve common disputes. The student teachers get academic credit, and many also come away with a better understanding of what people need to learn about the law.

For adults, community colleges, local school districts and college extension programs should offer more reasonably-priced courses on basic legal skills. In this area particularly, trained legal educators are sorely needed. The present practice of having these courses taught by under-employed lawyers prospecting for clients does less for the students than it does for the lawyer's business.

Finally, states should establish and publicize law-related education programs as part of their consumer protection activities. As part of these programs, they should:

☞ Publish and widely distribute consumer guides to basic state laws, from abortions to wills.

☞ Establish legal clinics and tenants' rights groups to foster legal self-education and assistance.

☞ Produce recorded legal messages callers can quickly dial up for practical legal information on topics such as marriage, divorce and credit.

Public legal education programs can produce a great deal of information per dollar spent. Funding could come from using a small percentage of fines collected from traffic violations—or from a portion of lawyers' bar association dues.

> *If you laid all of our laws end to end, there would be no end.*
>
> —MARK TWAIN

Reduce Auto and Home Repair Rip-Offs

MILLIONS OF CONSUMERS FALL VICTIM EACH YEAR TO DISHONEST OR INCOMPETENT AUTO REPAIR SHOPS AND HOME REPAIR CONTRACTORS. BAD SERVICE NOT ONLY WASTES TIME AND MONEY, BUT CAN ENDANGER LIVES. THE LEGAL SYSTEM HAS HAD LITTLE SUCCESS AT PREVENTING THESE PROBLEMS OR COMPENSATING RIPPED-OFF CONSUMERS.

The law provides penalties for outright fraud and false advertising, but it doesn't protect consumers from bad auto or home repairs. This is true despite the existence of state agencies, financed by millions of our tax dollars, that oversee the repair industry. Here's what's wrong with the current system:

☞ Few states certify the practical or business skills of auto mechanics or home repair and remodeling contractors.

☞ Typically, complaining to regulatory agencies is a waste of time. Most of them have little legal authority to do anything about consumers' main complaint: incompetence.

☞ It's usually impossible to find out which repair firms consistently do a lousy job. Some government agencies do accept complaints against individual auto and home repair firms for shoddy or incomplete work, but do not make them available to the public. Complaints are usually made public only if some legal violation—theft, fraud or failure to post a bond—is alleged. Charges of incompetence aren't enough.

This means that it's not until after the fact that consumers can judge the proficiency of the people who work on their cars or homes. By that time, the consequences may be miserable (if the work is done so poorly that they have to spend time and money having it done over) or even disastrous (if brakes aren't fixed properly or inferior materials are used for home repair).

Consumers who receive bad service or shabby treatment have virtually no place to go for help short of filing a lawsuit. Suing in small claims court, assuming the dollar limit is high enough to cover the claim, can be effective, but it's no substitute for getting the job done right in the first place or quickly corrected if a mistake is made.

What to Do

Public agencies should provide cost-effective regulation of home repair contractors and auto mechanics in the consumer interest. Here's how:

Require registration. People who do auto and home repair work should be required to register with the state so they can be located if a problem surfaces later.

Test and license. Only about one-third of the states license contractors who do general repair and remodeling work, and requirements for licensing vary widely. To protect the public against incompetence, states should require auto mechanics and contractors working on major home repair projects to pass practical tests demonstrating competence in the specific types of work they do. Competence in business skills should also be required, because many consumer complaints result from business incompetence rather than lack of knowledge of the trade.

> *Why did New Jersey get all the toxic waste dumps and California get all the lawyers?*
>
> *New Jersey had first choice.*

All auto and home repair firms should pay a yearly fee to the state to finance these programs.

Settle disputes out of court. States should investigate fraud complaints against mechanics and contractors and suspend licenses for illegal practices. For complaints of shoddy or incomplete work, states should establish impartial binding arbitration—a process in which an independent expert evaluates the work and makes a final decision based on the facts of the case. If a ruling favors a customer, the repair company should be required to pay promptly (including the cost of arbitration) or do the job over, on pain of having its license suspended.

Disclose complaints. To help consumers make informed decisions about whom to hire, states should disclose the exact nature of past and current complaints filed against a specific auto repair shop or home repair firm and the status or resolution of each complaint.

Compensate rip-off victims. A repair firm that does shoddy or fraudulent work may be out of business by the time an arbitration award is made. If so, individuals who can no longer collect should be compensated from a state fund. Part of the license fee charged contractors and mechanics should be used to raise the necessary money.

Produce brochures on consumer rights. States should provide consumers with booklets explaining how to choose auto and home repair firms and how to file a complaint. Brochures should include information evaluating the most common voluntary certification programs for mechanics and home builders, including which ones are most meaningful.

Resources

Help in Choosing a Contractor. The National Association of Home Builders (15th and M Streets, NW, Washington, DC 20005, (800) 363-5242) publishes a free brochure, *How to Choose a Remodeler Who's on the Level.* It covers how to select a home improvement contractor, protect yourself in a written contract and resolve disputes.

Help in Choosing an Auto Repair Shop. The Automotive Service Association (P.O. Box 929, Bedford, TX 76095, (800) ASA-SHOP), a nonprofit trade association serving the automotive repair industry, publishes several free brochures. They cover how to select auto repair firms in general as well as guides to specific types of auto repair, such as collision or brake repair.

Contracts for Home Remodeling. Simple Contracts for Personal Use, by Stephen Elias and Marcia Stewart (Nolo Press) includes sample contracts for home repair and remodeling to help assure that contractors get the work done right, on time and within budget.

How to Complain. Consumer's Resource Handbook (available free from the Consumer Information Center, Pueblo, CO 81009) provides general advice on how to file complaints against a business and choose auto repair and home remodeling services.

Compensation for Victims and State Programs. At least six states (Arizona, Connecticut, Hawaii, Maryland, Minnesota and Virginia) have funds to reimburse consumers who are victims of dishonest or incompetent contractors. To find out if your state has a similar recovery fund, contact your state's consumer protection office or Attorney General's office, listed in the government section of the phone book. The same agency can tell you if your state licenses or registers home improvement and auto repair firms, provides complaint information or publishes useful consumer materials.

Adopt Pay-at-the-Pump No-Fault Auto Insurance

PEOPLE WHO SURVIVE A CAR WRECK USUALLY FEEL FORTUNATE—UNTIL THEY BEGIN TO DEAL WITH THE LEGAL SYSTEM. THEN THEY QUICKLY REALIZE THAT THEIR TROUBLES HAVE JUST BEGUN. IN MOST STATES, THE SYSTEM THAT IS SUPPOSED TO COMPENSATE THE VICTIMS OF AUTO ACCIDENTS PRIMARILY BENEFITS LAWYERS, DOCTORS AND INSURANCE COMPANIES.

If you are injured in a car accident and believe it was the other person's fault, you start by contacting their insurance company (or your insurance carrier does it for you). This assumes, of course, the other driver is insured, which is by no means a given. Unless it's a relatively minor case, or one where the other person was flamingly at fault, chances are the insurer will not offer you a fair settlement.

At this stage, you probably need legal help. In evaluating whether or not to take your case, a lawyer will probably be only marginally concerned with what happened. Instead, the lawyer will focus on:

☞ How sympathetic a victim will you seem to a jury?

☞ How well-insured or wealthy are the parties you intend to sue?

☞ How much do you make? Professionals can sue for more

> *When the verdict in his first case was announced, the young lawyer rushed to call his senior partner. "Justice prevailed," he yelled into the phone. "Appeal, appeal," the partner replied.*

lost wages than warehouse workers can.

☞ Is your injury the type where medical expenses are high or can be easily padded? Doctors' and hospital charges will be tripled or quadrupled to compute the pain and suffering component of any award.

☞ How often does the opposing counsel for the insurance company settle cases out of court? If the other lawyer has a "fight to the death" reputation, it will be harder for you to find a lawyer.

If you don't have a cut-and-dried case, or the other person is uninsured, you may have trouble finding a lawyer who will help you. If your case looks promising and the lawyer agrees to represent you, your next step is to wait—and when you are done waiting, wait some more. The other person's insurance company doesn't have to pay a cent until your case is tried or settled, so it's got a strong incentive to delay.

Eventually, if no settlement is agreed to, you will be asked to go to court to relive in minute detail a brief, and perhaps tragic, event that took place years before. If no reliable eyewitnesses are available, the case may hinge on how you and the other driver describe what happened. This usually means all key parties will feel economic pressure to adjust their stories. Or, as more than one judge has put it, in a typical personal injury case, it's the jury's job to figure out who's lying the most.

Now it's time to wait for the jury's decision. If you found a decent lawyer, and the jury buys your story and not the other person's, you will win. You'll probably be awarded enough money to reimburse you for your medical bills and other out-of-pocket losses, plus about three times that amount as compensation for "pain and suffering." Your lawyer will take a third or more off the top for her services.

If you were unlucky in your choice of a lawyer, the jury isn't sympathetic or you can't locate a key witness, you'll get little or nothing. This is true even though you may have been horribly injured in an accident not your fault.

How does a system that's so obviously slow and unjust survive? Because it serves the interests of insurance companies and lawyers very well. Insurers make out the best by selling expensive auto coverage to individuals. A small portion of your premium dollar goes to pay accident victims, but much more of it ends up in the pockets of a good-sized army of agents, actuaries, managers and executives.

Personal injury lawyers, who also have an immensely profitable business, are next in line. They advertise widely (just check the yellow pages of your phone book), interview lots of potential clients and accept cases where the chance of a big pay-out is greatest. They then have the victims sign contingency fee contracts, allowing the lawyer to pocket a third or more of the total pay-off. (See Proposal #7, Regulate Contingency Fees, for how to clean up this racket.)

While we are talking about the role of lawyers, don't forget the tens of thousands hired to defend insurance companies. Because they usually bill by the hour, they have a strong incentive to keep the gravy flowing by prolonging cases. And, of course, the better they are at keeping money out of the pockets of injured people, the happier their clients—the insurance companies—are.

Then there are the doctors, chiropractors and other health professionals. Often egged on by defense lawyers anxious to exaggerate their clients' injuries, some of them overtreat and overbill.

The bottom line is shocking. According to columnist and author Andrew Tobias, after all the intermediaries siphon off their share, only about 37% of the money Americans spend for auto liability insurance actually goes to compensate victims.

What to Do

The best alternative is to adopt a no-fault compensation plan that would cover the medical bills and lost wages of all car accident victims, regardless of who was at fault.

"No fault" simply means that if you get hurt, you get paid. Under a genuine no-fault system, you can't sue the other drivers involved in the crash, and they can't sue you. If you get in an accident, you file a claim with your own insurance company. It pays for your medical bills and lost wages plus, in cases of serious injury, a modest amount for pain and suffering based on a formula somewhat similar to the one used in workers' compensation cases.

Court fights—and therefore, trial lawyers—are largely eliminated. Your insurance money goes to pay claims, not personal injury lawyers.

One of the most talked-about versions of no fault is called Pay-at-the-Pump Private No-Fault (PPN) auto insurance. It has been popularized by Andrew Tobias, whose best-known books are about personal investing. It is essentially a new way to collect insurance premiums. Instead of paying a lump sum insurance premium every year, you pay your insurance every time you buy gas—25¢ to 50¢ per gallon, with the lower amount charged in states like Montana, where most people must drive long distances. This way, every driver pays for auto insurance and every driver is covered.

Money would be collected by each state. Private insurance companies would then contract with the state to provide coverage and pay claims for groups of randomly selected motorists. The legions of insurance agents, who add much cost to the present system, would be eliminated. (For details about the plan, see Tobias' book, *Auto Insurance Alert!* or the 1994 California ballot initiative based on it.)

Rest assured that personal injury lawyers have recognized the threat no-fault poses to their wallets. At the same time, they have also had to recognize the growing popularity of this common sense plan. In a number of states, lawyers' groups have attempted to head off real reform by backing phony no-fault laws that preserve the right to sue for all but the smallest claims. Obviously, this approach stands logic on its head, since it's precisely for the larger claims where the insurance companies have the biggest incentive to resist making fair settlement offers.

Lawyers have also tried to nit-pick no-fault plans to death, claiming that since everyone pays the same mileage-based fee, bad drivers and accident-prone teenagers are subsidized by good drivers. Although some of these criticisms have some validity, none is convincing compared to the evils of the present system. For example, while it's true that teenagers have more accidents, and that the present system recognizes this by charging them more, it's also true that everyone is a teenager once, so viewed over time, paying a flat fee per gallon of gas works out fairly.

Lawyers also spend millions on public relations campaigns to convince us that it's dangerous to give up our day in court. Nonsense.

Four out of five doctors say that if they were stranded on a deserted island with no lawyers, they wouldn't need any aspirin.

The much-heralded "right to sue" for car accidents is a sham. Developed to serve a society of ox-carts and horse-drawn buggies, the adversary court system fails miserably in the age of mass automobile ownership and high-speed freeways, when it is often impossible even to determine who caused an accident.

The bottom line is simple. Adopting a well-designed no-fault system would mean that insurance premiums would go down and the lawyer lottery would be replaced by a humane system that compensates all injured people fairly. Everyone except lawyers and insurance companies would gain.

Make Judges Disclose Bias

A BIASED JUDGE CAN SWAY THE OUTCOME OF A JURY
TRIAL, AND ABSOLUTELY PREDETERMINE THE RESULT OF A
COURT TRIAL. BUT AMAZINGLY, A JUDGE'S BACKGROUND,
INVESTMENTS AND MINDSET ARE SELDOM DISCLOSED TO
THE PEOPLE INVOLVED IN A CASE.

No problem undermines the goal of a fair legal system more
than hidden judicial bias. In cases heard by judges alone—much
more common than jury trials—if a judge has a hidden bias, it is
very likely to unfairly determine the result.

Even in jury trials, judges make dozens of decisions about
the evidence presented by the parties and the tactics pursued by
the attorneys. They have the power to neutralize the objectivity
and fairness that the jury is supposed to provide.

Courts have long recognized that people can be consciously
or unconsciously influenced by biases. Before they are allowed to
sit on a jury, potential jurors are asked a series of questions
designed to root out possible favoritism. For example, potential
jurors for a landlord-tenant trial might be asked whether or not
they have ever been evicted.

When a possible bias is discovered during this questioning,
the judge and lawyers usually ask the potential juror whether he
or she can overcome it and render a verdict based only on the
evidence presented. If the answer is no, or the bias appears to be
so deep that no reasonable person could overcome it, the judge
will dismiss the juror outright. If the person claims to be able to
overcome the bias, the judge and attorneys may let the person

serve on the jury, depending on their assessment of the juror's sincerity.

This process ensures that people most likely to be biased will not serve as jurors in a case, and alerts the jurors already chosen to guard against letting their bias affect their decision.

A similar process is badly needed to expose judges' biases. Today, judges routinely hear cases in which they are at serious risk of being influenced by their personal prejudices, friendships, political debts and campaign contributions. Judicial bias may run from the creepingly subtle to the damningly blatant:

☞ A judge hearing a child support dispute may have just finished locking horns with an ex-spouse in a bitter battle over child support.

☞ A judge who is a landlord with a cynical attitude toward tenants may cheerfully preside over an eviction lawsuit.

☞ A judge who has received a campaign contribution from a lawyer may rule favorably on that attorney's cases or be tough on lawyers who supported an opponent.

Under current rules of ethics, judges are required to inform the parties and perhaps disqualify themselves from hearing a case only in three situations:

☞ they independently conclude that they can't be fair

☞ they have a financial interest in the outcome, or

☞ they are related to one of the parties or attorneys.

The reason judges are not subjected to the same stringent bias disclosure rules as are jurors is simple: Judges presume that they are wise enough and objective enough to be able to recognize and correct their own biases without oversight or disclosure. An occasional judge may be able to do this, but most, like the rest of us, cannot.

Judges don't ascend the bench because of demonstrated wisdom, insight and fairness. Most are appointed because they knew the right politician or were elected because of their ability to raise substantial campaign funds.

What to Do

To help ensure that a dispute headed for a trial will receive an unbiased hearing, the judge should fill in and distribute a two-part disclosure statement to all parties named in a case and the attorneys representing them.

Part 1 would require the judge to answer some basic questions, such as:

☞ Are you related to or acquainted with the parties or the lawyers in the case?

☞ Do you have outside knowledge of the facts in the case that would affect your ability to judge it fairly?

☞ Do you have any economic interest in the outcome of the case?

☞ Do you know of any other reason that might render you unable to be fair in the case?

The second part of the form would contain the same kind of questions that are put to jurors in a jury trial. It would elicit attitudes or information that might result in more elusive judicial bias in the type of case being tried. For instance, in a trial for medical malpractice, the judge and attorneys would likely agree that the judge should disclose if he or she:

☞ was related to a doctor who had been sued for malpractice

☞ had ever sued a doctor, or

☞ knew any victims of malpractice.

In this example, if the judge had sued a doctor for malpractice, the lawyer representing the hospital might reasonably conclude that the judge was biased against hospitals and request a different judge. As usually happens with biased jurors, a judge who decided that he or she could overcome this possible bias could legally remain on the case but at least proceed with some insight. But this decision could be the basis for an appeal if the party who complains about the bias could show that it substantially affected the judge's decision or behavior in the court.

This would not impose much of a burden on judges. In jury trials, with increasing frequency, judges question the jury themselves after meeting with the attorneys to formulate the basic questions. This type of meeting could be held in court trials as well, and in both kinds of trials the judge would answer the questions.

What do you call a lawyer with an IQ of 40?

Your honor.

Restructure Legal Aid

OUR COUNTRY WAS FOUNDED ON THE PRINCIPLE OF LAW
AND THE IDEAL OF JUSTICE FOR ALL. SADLY, BY SHUTTING
PEOPLE OUT OF THE CIVIL SYSTEM IF THEY CAN'T AFFORD A
LAWYER, WE MOCK THESE TENETS.

Over the last quarter century, poor people have gotten some
legal access through the federally-funded Legal Services Program. But despite the efforts of many committed people, the
results have been disappointing, in part because Legal Services is
inadequately funded. Most low-income people still go without
help for their day-to-day legal needs, with profound consequences. They have no way to get a divorce, set up a guardianship for a child, adopt a child or get help when threatened with
eviction.

Some people argue that the current $400 million Legal
Services program simply needs more money to be successful.
This is naive. It would take billions to hire all the lawyers and
support personnel needed to do the job—a sum that neither the
federal nor state governments
are likely to authorize anytime between now and the
year 3000.

Lawyers' groups unfail-
ingly claim that lawyers can
"close the gap" by providing
volunteer (pro bono) services.
But this commendable idea
has been tried repeatedly—

> *The law, in its
> egalitarianism, forbids
> the rich as well as the poor
> to sleep under bridges, to
> beg in the streets and to
> steal bread.*
>
> —ANATOLE FRANCE

and failed. Lawyers who contribute free services do make a difference. But when you try to spread their volunteer hours to the millions who need assistance, this approach is about as effective as dealing with the problem of world hunger by having the affluent dole out their table scraps.

More important, in any democracy worthy of the name, the poor shouldn't have to depend on charity for access to the legal system. Legal access should be available to all as a matter of right.

What to Do

There is a workable, affordable way to provide routine legal services to the poor: Set up neighborhood law clinics staffed by trained, competent non-lawyers. They could provide a wide range of legal services that are now unavailable to most low-income people, including help with probate, divorce, traffic tickets, wills and other problems.

Wouldn't this be giving low-income people second-rate legal help? Not at all. Most legal tasks undertaken in Legal Services offices are already handled, start to finish, by legal secretaries and paralegals. Indeed, even in prestigious private law firms, high-priced lawyers do next to none of the paperwork for routine actions. This makes good sense, because filing papers to get an uncontested divorce or bankruptcy, opposing an eviction or appealing a denial of unemployment benefits consists primarily of repetitive paperwork.

There is no reason to think that trained non-lawyers provide inferior services. Increasingly, middle-class consumers, unable to buy legal help from lawyers, are seeking out independent paralegals—non-lawyers who run their own offices, helping customers with legal paperwork. As Attorney General Janet Reno remarked in 1993 to the American Bar Association, non-lawyers provide cost-effective help with routine legal services such as divorces, bankruptcies, child support modifications and wills. Several bar-sponsored studies and investigations indicate that customers who hire independent paralegals to help with legal paperwork express a high level of satisfaction.

As many consumers have found out the hard way, hiring a lawyer is no guarantee of quality work. Lawyers do not learn to provide good quality basic legal services in law school, nor are they tested for this skill in bar exams. In fact, new lawyers in legal services offices learn how to deal with routine matters from the secretaries and paralegals who have done it for years, not the other way around.

If the middle class can increasingly gain access to routine legal information and form preparation by replacing lawyers with paralegals, why can't the poor? The principal reason is that it's currently illegal for non-lawyers to provide legal advice. Independent paralegals avoid prosecution for practicing law without a license by claiming that they are merely legal stenographers who type legal forms under the direction of their customers. Unfortunately, no such gray market argument will work for a full-service, government-sponsored legal clinic designed to bring a wide range of legal services to America's low-income areas. To allow paralegals to provide a broad range of legal services, the unauthorized practice laws must be abolished. (See Proposal #28, End the Lawyer Monopoly: Bring Competition to the Law Business.)

Staffing legal clinics with lower cost paralegals rather than lawyers will still cost plenty. With no significant new government funding in

> *In the law, the only thing certain is the expense.*
>
> —SAMUEL BUTLER

> *The minute you read something you don't understand, you can be almost sure it was drawn up by a lawyer.*
>
> —**WILL ROGERS**

the offing, a bootstrap approach will be necessary to pay for salaries, operations, training and other costs inherent in expanding this program.

Here's how to raise the money:

Existing federal funds. Paralegals will need a high level of training to provide excellent services (and to quiet lawyer critics). A substantial portion of the current $400 million budget of the Legal Services Program should be used to pay for classroom instruction, on-the-job materials, continuing education and monitoring neighborhood offices to be sure they are delivering top-notch services.

User fees. Beyond training, the biggest cost will be for staff salaries and day-to-day operating costs such as rent and office supplies. The bulk of these costs can be covered by charging customers modest fees. Non-lawyer legal typing services in California have demonstrated that many routine actions, such as bankruptcy and divorce, can be profitably handled for $100 to $200—an amount within the reach of many low-income people.

Tax lawyer services. Although many low-income people can pay for essential legal services if the cost is kept low, additional money will be required to provide legal help to those who can't afford to pay anything, and to fund larger lawsuits attacking the many unfair barriers our society inflicts on the poor. One method of raising needed funds, suggested by Robert Gnaizda of San Francisco's Public Advocates, is to tax legal services provided by big firms, much as other sales are taxed. No new tax is popular, but if this one were made at least a partial substitute for lawyers who did not have the time or energy to do pro bono work, many would likely support it.

Stop the Billion Dollar Rip-Off: Take Lawyers Out of House Sales

MORE THAN CAR CRASHES, MORE THAN DIVORCE, MORE THAN PROBATE, LAWYERS COLLECTIVELY FLEECE CONSUMERS OUT OF HUGE SUMS WHEN HOUSES ARE BOUGHT AND SOLD. AS HAS BEEN DEMONSTRATED IN CALIFORNIA AND OTHER STATES THAT ALLOW NON-LAWYERS TO HANDLE REAL ESTATE SALES, LAWYERS ADD NOTHING TO THESE TRANSACTIONS EXCEPT A BIG BILL.

When a house is bought or sold, the blanks and boxes on pre-printed contracts must be filled out and a title search conducted. Hiring lawyers to do this routine work is required by law and custom in most East Coast and midwestern states. Because two—and often more—lawyers are involved in every sale, and they do not come cheap, each year billions of dollars end up in lawyers' wallets.

Real estate professionals and title companies, who are involved with real estate issues every day and are tested and licensed, could easily handle this routine work as part of ample commissions and fees they are already paid. Proof of this can be found in California and several other states, where laws already allow trained non-lawyers to do this work. Consumers rarely hire lawyers during routine sales of residential property in these states, and there is absolutely no evidence they suffer legal problems as a result.

Why are non-lawyers prohibited from helping with buy-sell contracts and house closings in so many states? Because lawyer-influenced state legislatures make it so. In short, financially hard-pressed house purchasers have to pay an unnecessary lawyer tax for no other reason than that lawyers require it.

Not every house purchase or sale is simple, of course. What if a thorny legal issue is discovered—for example, a zoning problem or an unexpected lien or easement? Fine; legal help is always an option. An occasional problem is no reason to require every house purchaser and seller to pay thousands of dollars to lawyers.

What to Do

Here are some changes that would go far toward cleaning up the house-closing racket:

☞ Repeal all state laws and regulations that prohibit real estate professionals from handling house sale paperwork and have the effect of requiring lawyers.

☞ Require that all routine paperwork involved in house transfers be written in plain English. Documents should be accompanied by detailed and easy-to-understand materials describing the laws and customs involved in buying or selling a house.

☞ Require that title insurance policies be written to protect the buyer from problems with the title to the property. Currently, many policies protect only the lender from defects in title. Protecting the buyer this way would eliminate much of the risk of the transaction and reduce the need for lawyers.

No Lawyers Required in Washington State

Despite the financial interest of real estate lawyers and the huge sums they fling around state legislatures to keep the present system in place, reform of real estate laws in the consumer interest is definitely possible. For example, in 1985, the Supreme Court of Washington expressly recognized the lawyers' monopoly on real estate transactions for what it is: a consumer rip-off. Specifically, the court ruled that buyers and sellers had the right to choose a non-lawyer to handle the paperwork for a property transfer.

In the case, *Cultum v. Heritage House Realtors*, 694 P.2d 630, a real estate agent prepared a standard form purchase/sale contract for a customer who wanted to buy a house. The contract, originally drafted by a lawyer, contained boxes and blanks for information. The purchaser changed her mind about the house and sued Heritage House under Washington's Consumer Protection Law, seeking damages based on the agent's "unauthorized practice of law."

The Washington Supreme Court ended the lawyer monopoly by ruling that licensed real estate professionals who prepare house sale contracts are not practicing law. The court said:

> "For a long time, suppression of the practice of law by non-lawyers has been proclaimed to be in the public interest, a necessary protection against incompetence, divided loyalties and other evils....We no longer believe that the supposed benefits to the public from the lawyers' monopoly on performing legal services justifies limiting the public's freedom of choice. The public has the right to use the full range of services that brokers and salespersons can provide."

Simplify Bankruptcy

PEOPLE WHO GET INTO DEBT OVER THEIR HEADS ARE
OFFERED A SECOND CHANCE BY OUR BANKRUPTCY LAWS.
UNFORTUNATELY, THE BANKRUPTCY PROCESS IS MORE
COMPLICATED, EXPENSIVE AND LEGALISTIC THAN IT NEEDS
TO BE. AND TOO OFTEN, THE INTERESTS OF DEBTORS ARE
SACRIFICED TO THOSE OF LAWYERS.

Consumers can file for one of two types of bankruptcy. The
Chapter 7 bankruptcy system gives debtors a fresh start by
canceling (discharging) most of their debts. In exchange, some of
a debtor's property is sold, and the proceeds go to pay creditors
part of what they're owed. Chapter 13 bankruptcy is more
complicated. The debtor usually doesn't have to give up any
property, but must agree to pay a portion of the debts over
several years. In exchange, the rest of the debts are wiped out.
   Both forms of bankruptcy are handled in federal bankruptcy
court. Someone who files for bankruptcy need only fill out
several fairly-straightforward forms showing assets, debts,
income and expenses, and make a list of property the debtor
claims he or she is legally entitled to keep. Court appearances are
rarely required. Most debtors go to court only once—to answer a
few questions posed to them by a creditor or the bankruptcy
trustee, the official handling the case for the court.
   But because only lawyers are allowed to represent people in
federal court, debtors must either hire an attorney or handle
their case themselves. Going it alone is very difficult for people
who lack good reading skills or the requisite knowledge and self-

> *Litigation is a machine which you go into as a pig and come out as a sausage.*
>
> —AMBROSE BIERCE

confidence. In some communities—not many— they can get help with paperwork and filing from non-lawyer typing services for between $100 and $200 a case. Bankruptcy attorneys are engaged in a vigorous nationwide campaign to drive these non-lawyer services out of business.

As a result, most of the 600,000 people who file for bankruptcy every year end up hiring a lawyer to handle their paperwork and appear with them in court. Assuming a typical lawyer's fee is $600, and only about half of the cases are complex enough to require a lawyer's services, roughly $180 million is unnecessarily consumed by bankruptcy lawyers each year. Obviously, debtors could better spend that huge amount of money to repay creditors or help themselves start over.

What to Do

An administrative agency, staffed by bankruptcy experts, should be created to take the place of the bankruptcy court. Lawyers and courts should be eliminated except for relatively rare situations when there is a constitutional right for a dispute to be handled in court.

The new agency would:

☞ create user-friendly instructions to help people complete bankruptcy forms without professional assistance, and provide free guidance for those who need help

☞ check forms for completeness and accuracy before debtors filed them, and

☞ solicit any additional information needed from the debtor by telephone or mail.

As with the present system, notice of the bankruptcy filing would be sent to all creditors the debtor listed. The creditors could either examine the papers directly by using a computer, modem and telephone line, or receive a printout of the papers upon request. The creditors would be given a reasonable time to respond.

A bankruptcy examiner would then issue a proposed order based on the law and the information provided by the debtor and creditors. If the examiner concluded the debtor could repay the debts, the order would invite the debtor to submit a repayment plan. If not, the order would identify the debts to be canceled and the property to be sold.

If the debtor or a creditor disagreed with the examiner's order or wished to raise some other issue—such as whether a particular debt should be canceled—mediation services from a neutral third person would be available. If this failed, the dispute would be resolved in an informal administrative hearing.

Like the current bankruptcy court system, this new system would be funded by bankruptcy filing fees—which should be substantially reduced due to the new system's increased efficiency in handling routine bankruptcy cases.

> *Every seventh year you shall practice remission of debts. This shall be the nature of the remission: Every creditor shall remit the due that he claims from his neighbor; he shall not dun his neighbor or kinsman.*
>
> —Deuteronomy 15:1-2

Bankruptcy: It Can Happen to Anyone

Who files for bankruptcy, and why? According to a comprehensive study of consumer bankruptcy filings, bankrupt people are much like any of us—not exceptionally poor, not particularly reckless in their borrowing habits. The one characteristic they share is a recent, major disruption in income—caused by a job loss, small business failure or injury.

The truth is, lots of us are but a few missed paychecks away from bankruptcy.

For a unique view of the bankruptcy process, see *As We Forgive Our Debtors*, by Theresa A. Sullivan, Elizabeth Warren and Jay Lawrence Westbrook (Oxford University Press 1989).

Take Divorce Out of Court

GETTING DIVORCED IS A WRENCHING PROCESS, OFTEN
MADE WORSE BY INTRUSIVE, LENGTHY, EXPENSIVE AND
NEEDLESSLY HOSTILE LEGAL PROCEEDINGS. LAWYERS, WHO
PROFIT FROM THE MISERY OF DIVORCING COUPLES—THE
MORE FIGHTING, THE MORE PROFIT—HAVE RESISTED THE
FUNDAMENTAL REFORMS NECESSARY TO CIVILIZE THE
PROCESS.

Historically, the main problem with divorce proceedings has
been their preoccupation with fault. To get a divorce, spouses
must testify in court to often phony legal grounds, such as
"mental cruelty" or "desertion." This charade virtually mandates
perjury. Too often, it encourages acrimony and finger-pointing,
which in turn creates an atmosphere so poisonous that it makes
it difficult to cooperate in the future to raise children.

Many states have at least partially solved this problem with
no-fault divorce laws, which allow a couple to divorce without
first having to prove that one person was at fault. Unfortunately,
a number of states allow no-fault divorce only after a long
separation, or if there are no children—qualifications most
people don't meet.

Even in states that make no-fault divorce available to all,
getting a divorce can involve filing up to a dozen court forms
and going before a judge, often more than once. It's an intimidating process, especially to emotionally distraught couples. To
cope with the legal labyrinth, many people pay lawyers substantial fees.

The public regards lawyers with great distrust. They think lawyers are smarter than the average guy, but use their intelligence deviously. Well, they're wrong. Usually they're not smarter.

—F. LEE BAILEY

Another reason people facing a divorce run to lawyers is the mind-boggling complexity of laws concerning property ownership and division, child support, custody and visitation. Despite the fact that these laws cover fundamental legal rights, most of them are indecipherable by the average person. (See Proposal #19, Write Laws in Plain English.)

Lawyers, driven by the search for the almighty fee, typically charge divorcing spouses by the hour. It's easy for them to exploit people's inability to get good legal knowledge, by giving advice that prolongs the process. Although some lawyers are scrupulously honest, too many instigate or encourage aggressive legal maneuvers, delays and even perjured testimony, fostering arguments over custody, property division or spousal support. Given this kind of lawyering, even the most cordial of uncouplings can degenerate into a battle. A contested divorce can easily require 100 hours of attorney time on each side, for a total of 200 hours. At an average hourly rate of $150, that amounts to $30,000. And even if the lawyer for one side is a decent, humane sort, bent on keeping costs and animosity down, it will have little effect if the other spouse is represented by someone following a "take-no-prisoners" approach.

Yet another negative in the current system—one that also plays into the hands of litigation-happy lawyers—is that in some states judges have too much discretion to set child and spousal support levels and divide couples' property. Wherever similar cases can be decided differently, according to the whims and preferences of a particular judge, it doesn't take long for the word to get around. One judge is said to be hard on women while another is reputed to consistently award high child support. The result is that people feel the need to shop for a lawyer who is adept at manipulating the system, so that their case will come before the "right" judge.

What to Do

A few reforms are simple and obvious. They could be easily and quickly implemented, and start yielding benefits right away:

☞ Fault should be eliminated as a prerequisite for divorce in all states, no matter how long the couple has been separated and regardless of whether or not they have any children. Anyone who decides on divorce in his or her own heart should be free to end the relationship with dignity.

☞ Divorce laws themselves need to be easy to understand and widely publicized. Everyone, not just lawyers, should have access to the rules governing such a personal and important matter.

☞ Courts should, as much as possible, standardize rules for child support, child custody and alimony, and publicize them widely.

☞ Courts should make free, publicly-funded mediation, designed to head off disputes about child custody and visitation before they escalate, an integral part of the new system.

☞ For people without minor children or large amounts of property, the current court system could be largely replaced by a simple administrative process of de-registering marriages. To marry, you need only state your name, age and address, get a few simple medical tests and pay a small fee. When both parties are willing, divorce should be even easier—you don't need the tests.

No matter how we simplify and improve the divorce process, some divorces will still involve messy disputes over the fair division of property, custody of children or child support. But these disputes do not logically require, or benefit from, a complicated court-controlled process. Depending on the dispute, couples should be referred to various types of help outside of court. For example, instead of going before a judge who has little or no expertise in financial and tax matters, a couple having difficulty valuing property in order to divide it fairly could be referred to an approved financial planner, who could provide the help at a reasonable cost. Then the couple could return to the public administrator to complete the divorce.

What about the small percentage of divorce cases from hell—the ones where one, or both, parties are out to punish the other, as can occur when parents deliberately drag their children into their battles? What if one spouse attempts to intimidate, manipulate or even frighten the other into giving up valuable rights? To handle these and other serious problems, allow either party to request formal court review at any stage of the proceedings. That way, courts and judges would be there for those who need their power, but wouldn't interfere with people ready and able to take advantage of simpler approaches to end their marriages.

In a thousand pounds of law, there's not an ounce of love.

—ENGLISH PROVERB

Anatomy of a Rip-Off: The $40,000 Divorce

This is the true story of a woman who spent two years and more than $30,000 for a divorce—and was left with her original legal problem unresolved.

Jill and Sam had been married four years when Jill first consulted a lawyer. The couple had personal problems; Jill was also concerned because her husband refused to cooperate in filing income tax returns, and the IRS had begun actions against the couple.

The lawyer, Barbara, explained that a divorce could best protect Jill against tax liability. She said that the divorce could be handled by an inexperienced attorney in the firm, Jonas, under Barbara's supervision. Jill was assured that the case was simple—the couple had no children, owned little property jointly except a house and alimony wouldn't be an issue. Jill agreed and paid a $2,500 retainer.

Sam and Jill sold their house before the divorce papers were served, which netted a profit of $50,000 that belonged equally to both of them.

During the next few months, Jonas charged Jill about $3,000 for two routine legal tasks. Then Jill learned that Barbara—who supposedly had been supervising Jonas—had left the firm. Another partner, Elaine, said that she would supervise Jonas and implied that Jill's position in the case would suffer if Jill dumped the firm.

Elaine asked Jill to let the firm start a legal process known as "discovery," to find out whether Sam was concealing jointly owned assets. In discovery, each side makes the other produce documents, respond to written questions under oath and answer questions in person under oath and on record. Elaine estimated the cost of discovery at $2,500.

Jill didn't see the need. Sam didn't have a job, and as far as Jill knew, all his money came from an inheritance that was clearly his alone. But Elaine cautioned that Jill would never forgive herself if she later found that Sam had hidden assets to which Jill was entitled. Feeling overwhelmed, confused and pressured to make a decision that day, Jill consented.

Discovery ended up costing about $8,000, and never turned up any hidden property. One reason for the high cost was Jonas's inexperience; he made mistakes that required additional court appearances and new papers, and spent many more hours than a more experienced lawyer would have.

As Jill realized that Jonas was learning to practice law at her expense, she complained. The firm knocked $1,000 off a bill and promised more supervision.

A year and a half after Jill had hired the firm, she'd paid almost $13,000 in legal fees and costs, and neither the divorce nor the tax problems were any closer to resolution. Panicked, Jill tracked down Barbara, who agreed to supervise Jonas again for a fee.

Although neither Sam nor Jill thought there was much to fight about, the lawyers took extreme positions, in the name of negotiating strategy, and settlement proposals flew back and forth for months. These negotiations cost Jill another $17,000 in legal fees.

Finally, a court granted the divorce. Jill received her share of the profit from the house, her car and her half of the joint bank accounts. This was exactly what it always appeared she was entitled to receive—and what she and Sam had agreed to almost two years earlier. But the judgment left open the question of potential tax liability—the very problem that had led Jill to seek legal help.

After the divorce was final, Jill received a $15,000 cash settlement and a bill from the law firm for $14,043.53. This brought the bill for what should have been a routine divorce to over $40,000. Jill refused to pay the last bill; the firm threatened to sue but at the last minute dropped the last $14,000 fee. Jill could have gone to arbitration to request a partial refund of fees paid—but by then she'd had more than enough of attorneys.

Computerize the Law

COMPUTERS ARE POWERFUL TOOLS THAT COULD BRING LEGAL INFORMATION AND FORMS TO THE PUBLIC EASILY AND EFFICIENTLY, BUT THEIR PROMISE HAS LARGELY BEEN IGNORED. ONLY LAWYERS HAVE THE EXPERTISE—AND THE MONEY—TO USE MOST EXISTING LEGAL COMPUTER PROGRAMS.

Accomplishing a wide array of legal tasks—bankruptcy, incorporation, divorce or probate, for example—requires only understanding routine court procedures and preparing the right paperwork. The average person, given access to the right materials and instructions on how to fill them out, is perfectly capable of handling the job.

Unfortunately, getting the necessary information and instructions can be nearly impossible. Courts occasionally furnish standardized forms, but almost never provide instructions. Form books written for lawyers can be hard to find outside of a lawyer's office or law library—and even harder to use. Self-help law books may not cover the particular subject or may be too limited in an individual situation.

One way that these significant barriers to legal access could quickly be eliminated is by making the computer the great equalizer—the ultimate self-help law filing cabinet. Computer access to legal forms and information is no longer far-fetched. Evolving technology makes computerized storage and retrieval of huge amounts of material easier all the time. Programming techniques are already available to make the information and

> *Knowledge and human power are synonymous.*
>
> —Francis Bacon

forms readily accessible to the public in a variety of formats. And the information super-highway, which is rapidly being constructed, will soon be able deliver this material to people in their homes or offices easily and cheaply.

One company that runs a telephone legal advice service—TeleLawyer—relies on a menu-driven legal information database that quickly produces narrowly focused answers to a wide variety of legal questions. Self-help law programs designed for use on personal computers already help people make wills or trusts, incorporate their businesses, create partnership agreements, draft patent applications and write contracts. Self-help law books on other subjects are being transformed into electronic versions that allow the user to quickly find answers to specific questions. Lawyers regularly use software programs and specialized databases to do research and prepare documents.

What to Do

A computerized legal information and forms system should be available to the general public in courthouses, public libraries and over the mammoth computer network the Internet. A cornerstone of such a system would be easy-to-use, consumer-oriented databases. It can be done; some Arizona and Colorado courthouses already have computer kiosks that produce forms for simple divorce and small claims court cases.

People who just needed information could first choose a general topic. Then they would gradually narrow their search, proceeding through a series of menus, until they found the answers they needed. For instance, suppose Paul is getting a divorce and wants to find out whether he has to share his government pension with his spouse. He could simply look through a list (menu) of general subject areas. After selecting "divorce," he would be presented with a list of related topics. He would select "pensions" from this list and encounter a third menu with types of pensions. He would select the entry for his type of pension and receive a clear statement of the rule used by his state's divorce court for that type of pension.

This kind of system could also provide step-by-step help in completing a legal task. The computer would produce all necessary forms and provide instructions for filling them in and filing them.

If Paul wanted assistance with divorce paperwork, for example, he would call up the procedure part of the divorce database and be presented with the necessary forms. He could fill in the forms online or download the form-generating software to his computer. When necessary, he could use the help feature of the program to get line-by-line instructions. When he finished, Paul could print out the forms, as well as accompanying instructions for signing, serving and filing them.

Another approach would permit Paul to type in a plain-English question, such as: "Must I share my government pension with my wife if we divorce?" The computer would analyze this question (a process called parsing) and determine that Paul wants information about pensions and divorce. The computer might then ask Paul to describe his pension, what state he lives in, how long he's been married, and possibly other questions. These answers would also be analyzed.

Implementing a self-help legal computer system will, of course, be harder than describing it. Expect little help from lawyers, who currently monopolize legal information and have seen to it that forms and instructions are rarely available, even for the simplest task.

Self-help law systems could, however, be profitable to the business that developed them. They could be sold to courts, libraries and online database vendors, which in turn could charge reasonable user fees.

A comprehensive system such as the one described here doesn't exist yet largely because of a lack of imagination. Business people, like so many others, think of law as something that belongs to lawyers. This will change. As legal software programs, such as those already on the market, proliferate and succeed, business will see the opportunity to profit. Along the way, computers could revolutionize public access to the legal system.

How many lawyers does it take to change a light bulb?

How many can you afford?

Eliminate Race, Gender and Other Prejudices From the Courts

IN THEORY, OUR COURTS ARE DEDICATED TO THE IDEAL OF FAIRNESS AND EQUAL TREATMENT FOR ALL WHO ENTER. BUT TOO MANY JUDGES BRING TO THE COURTROOM THE SAME PREJUDICES THAT TAINT OUR LARGER SOCIETY.

Corrosive as prejudice is in society, it is intolerable in the courts, where all citizens must seek justice. A few examples:

☞ A number of studies have found that the severity of a prison sentence is correlated with the race of the criminal's victim. Someone convicted of killing a white person, for example, usually gets a stiffer sentence than someone who kills a person of another race.

☞ One Texas judge justified giving a light sentence to a convicted killer because the victim had been gay. Many commentators criticized the judge's candor, but not his prejudice.

☞ Judges often treat minority and women witnesses, court employees and lawyers without respect. For example, one California judge ordered an attorney—the only woman among a group of seven—to type up a settlement agreement. "Come on sweetheart," urged the judge, "I know you can type."

☞ African-American and Hispanic lawyers are often harassed by court officers who assume they are criminal defendants. Judges sometimes call them by their first names and refer to minority clients as "boys" or "girls."

Such anecdotal evidence is well supported by systematic research. Recent studies, for example, found pervasive gender discrimination in New York, Massachusetts, New Jersey, Rhode Island, Maryland, Nevada and California courts. The result is "more than hurt feelings," the Massachusetts study concluded. These attitudes "affect women's ability to function in the system, and they are linked to unjust outcomes."

Prejudice destroys faith in the fairness of the court system. A 1989 New York investigation into racial bias found that many minorities mistrust the state's court system, which, of course, is overwhelmingly dominated by whites. In New York City Housing Court, for example, 81% of the tenants are black, but 79% of the judges are white. One woman asked the New York panel to imagine how a black mother feels when she goes into Family Court and sees white clerks, white guards, white psychologists, white correctional officers, white lawyers and white judges.

But despite the mounting evidence of bias, most courts refuse even to acknowledge the problem. This hypocrisy and indifference, on top of the unfairness directly caused by prejudice, make a travesty of the legal system's claims to provide equal justice under the law.

What to Do

To eliminate bias based on race, gender and ethnicity in the courts is a huge task—probably an impossible one, because courts are run by the same imperfect humans who bring the problem to other areas of American life. Add to this the fact that

> *There are two kinds of lawyers: those who know the law and those who know the judge.*

the legal establishment has always been conservative, revering tradition and loathing change.

But because each courthouse is a world unto itself, the situation isn't hopeless. And there is even an obvious place to start the reform process: with judges. Since judges, the majority of whom are white males, exert top-down control over the entire court system, changing their behavior would do much to set the tone for treatment of people who appear in court.

Start the reform process by appointing more minority members and women to the bench. As evidenced by Ruth Bader Ginsberg's selection to serve on the U.S. Supreme Court, the appointment of strong-minded people to key positions can make an immediate difference.

It's also essential to get more minorities into key, non-judicial positions in the justice system. The people who work as clerks, bailiffs, counselors and other court workers have the most direct contact with the public. If they are broadly representative of the people who use the courts, many racial and gender insensitivities will disappear.

But waiting years for the appointment of enough women and minority judges and other court personnel to make a difference isn't acceptable. Today's judges and other court employees should be taught to recognize and deal with invidious discrimination. Just as judges attend seminars to keep up on the law, they should regularly participate in programs to educate and remind them about how to protect the civil rights of all people who appear in their courts. Members of the minorities who face discrimination should be actively involved in helping to design the curriculum and teach the workshops.

What's Wrong & How to Fix It

An occasional seminar isn't, in itself, enough to change behavior. To reinforce the message that discrimination won't be tolerated, a California commission investigating the problem of bias has recommended that judges be given a "fairness manual," covering appropriate behavior toward jurors, employees and other people who appear in court. That's a great idea.

Finally, to deal with people who simply refuse to stop discriminating behavior, court rules should require judges to reprimand and, if necessary, discipline clerks, lawyers and others who make racist, sexist or other offensive comments or otherwise engage in discriminatory behavior. Judges who themselves violate these rules should be disciplined by state or federal judicial oversight agencies, and in serious cases, fired.

The thing to fear is not the law, but the judge.

—RUSSIAN PROVERB

Write Laws in Plain English

READING MOST STATUTES IS LIKE WADING THROUGH A SWAMP. AT EVERY STEP, MUDDY LANGUAGE PULLS AT YOU, AND THORNY CROSS-REFERENCES THREATEN TO TEAR YOU FROM YOUR PATH. MANY PEOPLE DON'T KNOW THEIR RIGHTS AND CAN'T PARTICIPATE IN THE LEGAL SYSTEM BECAUSE THEY CAN'T UNDERSTAND THE LAWS AS THEY ARE WRITTEN.

Most laws are written by lawyers. They excuse their mysterious legal jargon by claiming that the law is complex and requires special terms to convey its meaning precisely. But anyone who's ever tried to make sense of a statute knows that such legalese fosters confusion instead of reducing it. Poorly written statutes spawn lawsuits, where lawyers argue at length about what the words mean.

Sometimes legal terms are useful shorthand—but we're not talking about nuclear engineering manuals here. These are the laws that regulate our lives. Obscure terms are rarely necessary, and could always be explained in plain English somewhere in the statute.

The problem with the way most statutes are written is not only that they are full of unfamiliar terms; it's also that they are written poorly.

Here's an example, a Maryland law:

"The Board may appoint, discharge at pleasure, and fix the compensation of the secretary and such clerical force as from time to time in its judgment may be necessary in the adminis-

> *The statute books are exceedingly muddled. I seldom look into them.*
>
> —JUDGE MATHEW B. BEGBIE

tration of this subtitle if it has funds available for the payment of such persons."

The same law, as rewritten into plain English by a group that's tackling the whole set of Maryland statutes: "The Board may employ a staff in accordance with the state budget."

Laws written so that ordinary people can't understand them don't square with what we all learn, from grade school on: that we are responsible for knowing the law. And we *are* responsible, even if the law is incomprehensible. Just try telling a court clerk that you missed a crucial filing deadline because your state's law is written so poorly.

There are three main reasons why most laws read like hieroglyphics.

The first reason is rooted in a belief shared, perhaps unconsciously, by lawyers and legislators: that it doesn't matter that non-lawyers can't read the laws. Many of those who write laws simply assume that someone who wants to know what the law means will ask a lawyer. The legal profession gains much of its status—and profit—from its exclusive access to legal knowledge.

Second, bad writing begets bad writing. Law students learn legal writing by reading the jargon-filled decisions of judges. Imitating that sorry style, they are soon turning out prose packed with "said," "heretofore" and as much Latin as they can come up with.

Third, lobbyists and legislators who have lost a legislative fight over a law may actually want it to be ambiguous. If the wording in a statute is unclear, they may get another chance to argue over its meaning in a later lawsuit.

It should go without saying that people shouldn't have to rely on lawyers, paying through the nose or depending on uncertain charity (free legal services are only sporadically available and only to the very poor), to find out about the law that governs their lives. In a democracy, the laws belong to all. They are written by the legislators we elected. They should be written in the language we speak.

Legal commentators have wrung their hands for years over the poor quality of lawyers' writing, and law professors have proposed new scientific, computer-aided systems for drafting coherent statutes, but states have taken few steps toward making the laws comprehensible.

A few state legislatures have passed "plain English statutes," but these promising-sounding laws don't apply to the statutes they write themselves. Instead, they require certain kinds of consumer contracts to be written in clear, understandable language. Although commendable, these laws are so limited—many exclude mortgages, deeds and insurance policies—that their practical effect is insignificant.

And more than 20 years ago, President Carter directed federal agencies to make their regulations "as simple and clear as possible." The agencies hired consultants to help, but if federal regulations have become models of clarity, it has escaped most readers' notice.

What to Do

The solution is so simple that only politicians could miss it: Write our federal, state and local laws and regulations in plain English, so the average person can understand them. Some states have already taken small steps in this direction. California, for example, recently rewrote its small claims court laws to make them understandable to the average person. The task was supervised by the state Department of Consumer Affairs.

All laws, before lawmakers vote on them, should be scrutinized to make sure they are clear, unambiguous and written in everyday language. This wouldn't require adding a costly layer of bureaucracy to the legislative process. Most state legislatures already have a central office for bill-drafting. It shouldn't cost much to shift its priorities toward clarity and cogency.

To guide the people charged with overseeing bill-drafting, a national, nonpartisan citizens' committee should be created. Its job would be to write, publish and distribute common-sense guidelines for legislation. It should establish rules for sentence and paragraph length (statutes are notorious for going on and on and on), vocabulary (you shouldn't need a legal dictionary), grammar and syntax. It could also publish model laws, not for substance but as examples of clear expression.

Finally, there should also be a way for citizens to complain about garbled laws that slip through the system. Complaints could be referred to the bill-drafting committee, which would re-evaluate the clarity of the legislation.

Imagine the appeals

Dissents and remandments

If lawyers had written

The Ten Commandments

—HARRY BENDER

Make Competent Interpreters Available

PEOPLE WHO CANNOT SPEAK ENGLISH AND FIND THEMSELVES IN COURT ARE OFTEN AT THE MERCY OF UNQUALIFIED INTERPRETERS. IF THEY CANNOT UNDERSTAND OR PARTICIPATE IN WHAT IS GOING ON, A FAIR PROCEEDING IS IMPOSSIBLE.

Providing a skilled interpreter is critical to a fair legal proceeding. By controlling much of what the defendant, jury, judge and lawyers hear, an interpreter becomes the most powerful person in the courtroom—the only link between a non-English-speaking witness or party and everyone else in the courtroom. A bad job of interpreting can mean that a person loses custody of a child or valuable property, is deported or goes to jail.

Only criminal defendants are legally entitled to interpreters. And that legal requirement is frequently ignored. When a Cuban immigrant recently took the stand in his own behalf in a cocaine trafficking charge, the Los Angeles trial judge repeatedly bullied him to "try it in English." The judge cited efficiency. Testifying in his own language with the aid of an interpreter, according to the judge, would take twice as long as needed.

For civil actions such as divorces, there is no legal mandate for courts to provide interpreters. Non-English speakers must bring to court a relative or friend who can help out.

> *The language of the law must not be foreign to the ears of those who are to obey it.*
>
> —JUDGE LEARNED HAND

When an interpreter is used, courts do little to ensure that he or she is competent. The pay is not high enough, in many places, to attract skilled people. Only a few states and the federal courts require court interpreters to have passed a skills test; most courts do not require any evidence of interpreting skill.

At most, courts require basic knowledge of languages. But language experts protest that interpreting is a skill all its own, and being bilingual is no guarantee of interpreting ability. Interpreting, according to a professor who heads the country's first college program for legal interpreters, involves the tricky feat of communicating across culture. Interpreters must not only faithfully translate word-for-word, but are also required to come up with accurate translations of idiomatic expressions and readings of mood or inflection. Courtroom interpreters often have the additional burden of translating something often dubbed a language all its own: legal terminology.

Many untrained interpreters commit the cardinal sin of summarizing testimony—editing out offensive words, adding their own twists and skipping over difficult words. The frequent result is a significant change in the meaning or implication of what is said. Few of the many mistakes are caught. Even then, there is usually no recourse against a judgment that is already final.

Because qualified courtroom interpreters are in short supply, courts often find interpreters on a hit-or-miss basis. Sometimes they rely on bilingual court personnel. Sometimes they are more creative. One court clerk, for example, called Chinese restaurants until she found someone to interpret. "He was awfully hard to understand," she observed later.

But once an interpreter is working in a courtroom, it's rare that anyone present has the skills to evaluate ability or catch mistakes.

What to Do

Courts should make competent interpreters available for all proceedings, civil and criminal. And the interpreters should be paid salaries that reflect the skills required and importance of the service they provide.

Courts should employ only interpreters who present objective evidence of competency, such as a proof of passing a rigorous exam. Exams should be tough enough to ensure the competency of those who pass. The exams should emphasize practical interpreting skills, not just rudimentary language abilities.

To ensure a supply of competent interpreters, states should set up certification programs. They should also set standards for training programs, which could then be offered by public and private schools. Training should both teach translating skills and instill in students the ethics of the job—for example, that summarizing a speaker's testimony is a serious violation of an interpreter's responsibilities.

Finally, the state agency in charge of testing and certifying interpreters should regularly monitor the courtroom performance of certified interpreters.

> *It's better to enter the mouth of a tiger than a court of law.*
>
> —CHINESE PROVERB

Help Non-Lawyers Use Law Libraries

MANY LAW LIBRARIES ARE OFF-LIMITS TO NON-LAWYERS, AND ALL ARE NEEDLESSLY HARD FOR NON-LAWYERS TO USE. WITHOUT ACCESS TO A GOOD, USABLE LAW LIBRARY, THE PUBLIC CANNOT HAVE ACCESS TO LAW.

The average person needs dozens of legal questions answered in a lifetime. We may dispute tree ownership with a neighbor, child custody with a former spouse, or last year's taxes with the IRS. Or we may just need to know how to write a valid will, file for divorce or incorporate a small business. The best place to find specific answers is usually the law library.

Unfortunately, it is often impossible for non-lawyers to use this essential information source. For if law libraries own the law, lawyers own the law libraries. In some places, this is literally true: Lawyers rent the building, buy the books, and for the most part keep the public out. Even law libraries that are publicly funded—in courthouses or public law schools—are run primarily as a resource for law students, lawyers and judges.

Many law libraries, reflecting the elitist attitudes of their lawyer patrons, offer the public no assistance in how to approach the forbidding-looking books. They simply assume that anyone who wants to use the law library already possesses the research skills to track down and make sense of a large body of legal information. But because this arcane skill is taught only in law schools, everyone else is denied access to legal information.

> A *library is not a luxury,*
> *but one of the necessaries of*
> *life.*
>
> —HENRY WARD BEECHER.
> AMERICAN CLERGYMAN

The double standard is often manifested in how library privileges are allotted. Word processing rooms, conference areas and telephones—all extremely helpful in researching and preparing documents—are available to lawyers in many places, but off-limits to self-helpers. Similarly, many law libraries allow lawyers to check out books freely, but demand a deposit from non-lawyers before trusting them with materials.

The bias toward lawyers also shows up in the materials in the library's collection. Almost always, libraries are full of form books and practice manuals written for lawyers, but noticeably lacking in good self-help books and software.

What to Do

A number of simple reforms would help give citizens meaningful access to law libraries.

Start with the librarians in public libraries, who are often asked legal questions. They should be educated about the materials available at law libraries and how non-lawyers can use them.

All law libraries that receive public funds or subsidies, including those run by private colleges, should be open to the public. At law school libraries, students in Advanced Legal Research classes could get course credit for helping self-helpers use the library. Students would have to help someone with a specific legal research project. Students would get practical experience, and the self-helpers would get free assistance.

Every county—or every two or three counties in sparsely-populated areas—should have at least one public law library. These libraries should be open a reasonable number of evening and weekend hours. In larger law libraries, the reference staff should include at least one specialist to assist non-lawyers.

Public law libraries, many of which are chronically strapped for cash, should be funded from consistent, predictable sources. Typically, a percentage of lawsuit filing fees collected is allocated to the local courthouse library. But since lawyers benefit most from law libraries, they should provide a significant amount of the funding. A portion of their annual state bar association dues could be earmarked for public law libraries.

Law libraries should also be redesigned so that the public can more easily use them. Librarians should:

☞ Create pamphlets, displays, videos and other material to explain how legal materials are organized and catalogued.

☞ Prepare "fast track" outlines of how to do legal research on common problems, such as getting a divorce, increasing child support or coping with a landlord who won't make necessary repairs.

☞ Offer short courses on how to use the library, including tours and hands-on exercises.

☞ Gather together self-help software and books on disk and provide a computer or two for library users.

☞ Help library users locate free, useful legal information on the Internet.

> *Lawyer: One skilled in circumvention of the law.*
>
> —AMBROSE BIERCE

Using the Law Library

Here are some good tools to help you use the law libary. Most are in large law libraries.

Legal Research: How to Find and Understand the Law, Stephen Elias and Susan Levinkind (Nolo Press). A nontechnical but detailed book, written for non-lawyers. It's especially good on helping you frame research questions and get around the jargon trap.

Legal Research and Writing: Some Starting Points, William P. Statsky (West Publishing). This easy-to-use book contains photographs of law books and simple descriptions of how to use them.

How to Find the Law (9th Ed.), Cohen, Berring and Olson (West Publishing) and *Fundamentals of Legal Research,* Jacobstein and Mersky (Foundation Press). These texts are written for law students and may overwhelm you with detail. Each has a paperback abridgement that contains selected chapters.

The Process of Legal Research: Successful Strategies, Christina L. Kunz (Little Brown). An interesting feature of this book is that librarians discuss how to solve model problems.

Legal Research Made Easy, Robert Berring (Nolo Press/ Legal Star). This $2^{1}/_{2}$ hour videotape, designed for non-lawyers, shows you step-by-step how to formulate a legal research question and use the library to find the answer.

Feb up

Expand Small Claims Court Limits

AMERICA'S TRIAL COURT SYSTEM IS COSTLY, CONSTIPATED AND COMPLICATED BEYOND REASON. SMALL CLAIMS COURT, WITH ITS SIMPLE RULES, LOW COST AND EASY, FAST ACCESS FOR NON-LAWYERS, IS A POWERFUL ALTERNATIVE.

Especially when the small claims system is combined with a mediation program that encourages people to settle their cases outside the courtroom, it offers high-quality justice at a reasonable cost. But unrealistically low dollar limits and restrictions on the types of cases allowed in small claims court hobble its usefulness.

Small claims court offers people a chance to participate directly in their own cases. This fundamentally democratic aspect of the process is popular with most participants. And directly experiencing the problems, imperfections and ambiguities of presenting their cases often affords them a more realistic view of how our legal system works, as compared to a formal court, where most people participate secondhand through lawyer surrogates. Few participants in small claims court end up concluding that "I was robbed."

The great majority of common, everyday disputes are easy to understand and require relatively little money to resolve. These include spats over auto and home repairs, landlord-tenant problems, unpaid bills and substandard services. It's not worth the time or money to take these disputes to regular court. With attorney fees routinely running upwards of $150 or $200 per hour, a dispute must be worth at least $20,000 before it becomes cost-effective to hire a lawyer. If it's any less, the costs of resolving the problem—including lawyers' and court fees—loom larger than the problem.

The very act of bringing in lawyers, no matter what their cut, may ill serve the cause of justice. According to California Superior Court Judge Roderic Duncan, "People are much more likely to stand up and tell the unvarnished version of what happened when they represent themselves. Something about a lawyer being in the process, coaching people to alter their stories, results in victory becoming more important than telling the truth."

Less lying isn't small claims court's only virtue. Because nit-picking formal rules of evidence are relaxed, a judge can consider all evidence the parties present, which often produces a more just result. For example, in a landlord-tenant dispute, a small claims judge can read a building inspector's report if either party requests it. By contrast, in a regular court, the report might be rejected under formal rules of evidence unless the building inspector were present to testify to its authenticity, often a practical impossibility.

Unfortunately, because of ridiculously low dollar limits ($3,000 or less in most states), people with claims worth between $3,000 and $20,000 face a miserable choice. They can kiss off a good chunk of their potential recovery by reducing their claim to the small claims court maximum, try to represent themselves in a regular lawyer-controlled trial court, or hire a lawyer and take the risk that the fees charged are likely to be more than what they win.

Assume, for example, that a homeowner and a contractor disagree about whether a $20,000 kitchen remodeling job was done properly. Angry words are exchanged, and attempts to compromise prove futile. Each person hires a lawyer and the case goes to trial two years later. The lawyers each bill for 40 hours of time at $175 per hour, costing each side $7,000. Court fees, document preparation and expert witness fees add another $1,000 each. Assume now that the homeowner wins a partial victory—he need only pay the contractor $14,000 for the substandard work. Add that to the $8,000 in legal expenses, and the homeowner is out $22,000. The contractor fares little better, netting only $6,000 out of the $20,000, once legal fees are paid. In short, both sides lose, and spend needless hours and energy fighting in the process.

If the same case were brought in a small claims court with a strong mediation program, both the homeowner and contractor would have a much better shot at justice. Filing fees would amount to about $25, and each side could choose whether or not to spend a few hundred dollars to have the kitchen work evaluated by an expert witness. The case would then be promptly sent to a mediation program. With the help of an experienced mediator, there would be a good chance of the parties agreeing to a settlement.

If mediation failed, the case would be heard in small claims court within six weeks of filing, with each side getting the chance to have its say and present evidence. By keeping costs low, both parties would benefit almost no matter what the small claims judge decided. For example, even if the judge only knocked 10% off the contractor's bill, as opposed to 30% in the scenario above, the homeowner would pay a total of $18,000 plus a few dollars in fees as opposed to $22,000.

What to Do

The small claims court dollar limit should be raised to $20,000 in every state—an amount high enough to allow most consumer and small business disputes to be resolved in court without lawyers.

Simplified small claims procedures should also be made available for many more types of cases, not just those involving money, as is true in most states today. For example, if it's appropriate, a small claims judge should be allowed to order a neighbor to remove a dangerous tree or tell a tenant who doesn't pay the rent to vacate an apartment.

Lawyers should be banned from small claims court (as they already are, in some states), except when appearing for themselves.

Every court should provide a quick, easy-access mediation alternative right in the courthouse. Maine, which already does this, reports that over 50% of contested cases are settled by the parties themselves, with the help of a mediator. And happily for money-starved state governments, paying a mediator (who need not be a lawyer) is much cheaper than paying for a judge and running a courtroom. Even a free mediation system will quickly save taxpayers' money.

Finally, consumers should be better educated about how to use small claims court through self-help pamphlets, audiotapes and videos available from the court clerk. An in-person advisor program, like the one currently in place in California, could greatly aid those using the courts. These programs could be funded at no taxpayer cost by slightly increasing the fee to file a small claims case.

The California Small Claims Advisor Program

When a small claims court case is filed in California, a few dollars of the filing fee go to the small claims advisor program. In more populous counties, a trained consumer advocate provides free counseling to any person involved in a small claims suit. In rural counties, phone-in counseling is provided.

Small claims court advisors, who are particularly helpful to first-time filers, counsel both plaintiffs and defendants on how to research the law, prepare evidence and appear in court. The success of this program in helping inexperienced litigants was an important factor in the California legislature's decision to raise the small claims dollar limit to $5,000.

Privatize Civil Courts

THE U.S. CONSTITUTION GUARANTEES CRIMINAL
DEFENDANTS A SPEEDY TRIAL, BUT THERE IS NO SUCH
GUARANTEE FOR PEOPLE INVOLVED IN CIVIL CASES, WHICH
TYPICALLY DRAG ON FOR YEARS. FILE A CIVIL LAWSUIT
TODAY, AND IT MAY TAKE A YEAR—OR FIVE YEARS—TO
GET TO TRIAL. NOT ONLY DOES SUCH DELAY CAUSE
NEEDLESS INCONVENIENCE AND ANXIETY, IT SEVERELY
IMPAIRS OUR COURTS' ABILITY TO DO JUSTICE.

Urban courts are big businesses, many with up to 50 or
more courtrooms operating simultaneously. On a typical day,
everything from divorces to securities fraud cases must be heard.
Just getting the right people to the right room is daunting.
Making the whole system run efficiently is even more difficult.

Long delays have become a standard feature of civil lawsuits,
for several reasons. One is that courts and the bureaucracies that
come with them are administered by judges, people who were
appointed or elected to their positions for reasons that have
nothing to do with administrative skills or training. Another is
that courts, like many other large public bureaucracies, have
developed a heavy load of inefficient work habits. From the
clerk's office to the courtroom, time and money are frittered
away on trying to improve systems that should have been buried
when Eisenhower was president.

Unfortunately, the fact that our civil courts are obviously
failing has not triggered major reforms, such as hiring experi-

enced administrators to run things. Instead, judges, afraid that administrators would try to rein in their many perks and privileges, continue to claim a constitutional right to run things in their own way, no matter how inefficient. The fact that experience amply demonstrates that most are miserably equipped to do so matters not a whit.

The problem of poor judicial administration isn't limited to how and when judges work. Delay and inefficiency are built into every cranny of the trial court system. The arcane, history-encrusted rules of evidence and procedure upon which the system is based almost guarantee that the process will take too long and cost too much.

And then there are the lawyers. Especially when paid by the hour, as is common, lawyers have a motive for pokiness that is as obvious as it is insidious. And because the court process is convoluted, lawyers have dozens of chances to stretch out the process, all the while virtuously claiming that every objection, motion, discovery procedure and brief is essential to protecting the client's interests.

When lawyers work on a contingency fee basis—meaning that they get paid only if and when their clients win—you'd think they would move faster. After all, the sooner the case concludes, the sooner they get paid. But even here, lawyers are frustratingly slow. This time the reason is often psychological—many lawyers hate the hard work and stress of trials. Better to fill up a few years with routine and often worthless motions, until insurance company lawyers can convincingly claim they have delayed payment as long as possible and are willing to settle out of court.

> *Suits at court are like winter nights, long and wearisome.*
>
> — THOMAS,
> ENGLISH BALLAD WRITER

Another reason why our courts can't cope with their caseloads—and one that is out of the control of judges—relates directly to the many political decisions to get tough on crime. Every time legislators create another way for people to go to jail, judges have more criminal work to do and less time for other cases. The "war on drugs" alone has swamped the judicial system, just as it has overwhelmed police and prisons. The result is that, in some courts, judges now spend up to 80% of their time handling the criminal side of their dockets. Civil cases, which get lower priority, are pushed aside.

What to Do

For at least the past 20 years, a plethora of learned studies and prestigious commissioners have proposed all sorts of changes designed to speed up the court process. It has been widely recognized by reformers that courts could handle a much larger volume of work far faster if they hired skilled administrators and adopted modern managerial techniques. Although there have been some small successes, on balance, the many efforts to get the courts to reform themselves have been a failure.

A better approach would be to privatize large chunks of our civil court system. To an extent, this has already been done, as businesses and groups with the financial wherewithal opt for alternatives to court, including arbitration, mediation and the services of private judging companies. These private systems hire retired judges as decision-makers, but are administered by professional managers. Using tight deadlines and streamlined procedures, they have produced impressive results—so much so that private judging has become a true growth industry.

These programs are often run by entrepreneurs looking to make a big profit. The result is that only businesses and the affluent can afford to escape the public courts. In the long run, our democracy will be poorly served if the well-heeled can buy their day in an efficient private court, while everyone else still must wait years at the old inefficient county courthouse.

Far better to privatize the whole system by contracting with one, or several, private providers to handle all or most civil actions. For example, ABC county could ask for bids from private companies to handle all landlord-tenant, probate and personal injury cases. As part of the bid process, sensible parameters could be established to assure good quality. Private judging companies, who could either operate out of public facilities or set up their own, could bid for all or just one of these areas.

Because private companies would have an economic incentive to be efficient, the new system would almost surely be simpler and faster. Because it would also free governments from the choking financial responsibility to operate public courtrooms, it would be cheaper.

Nevertheless, some critics will likely argue that a purely private system doesn't give the average person the traditional right of a day in court. To cope with this, one approach would be to give litigants a choice to stick with a scaled down public system or use the private alternative. If the recent rush by business people to escape the expense and delay of the public courts is any guide, there is little doubt which most will choose.

> *When a lawyer becomes a judge, he no longer has a direct financial incentive to manipulate The Law in favor of the rich people and the big corporations. But he will usually have spent most of his professional life, before he became judge, doing just that...Which means that he will lean toward the side where the money lies—and The Law will lean with him.*
>
> —FRED RODELL, YALE LAW SCHOOL PROFESSOR

Do Away With Punitive Damages

THOUSANDS OF BUSINESSES HAVE CLOSED OR CURTAILED OPERATIONS BECAUSE THEY FEAR LAWSUITS AND CAN'T AFFORD LIABILITY INSURANCE. MORE WORRISOME, THE FEAR OF HUGE PUNITIVE DAMAGES AWARDS HAS KEPT POTENTIALLY USEFUL NEW PRODUCTS OUT OF THE U.S. MARKETPLACE.

In a personal injury case, the jury must decide whether the person being sued, the defendant, caused the victim's injury. If the defendant is found liable, the next question is how much money is needed to compensate the victim. The defendant is ordered to pay that amount, called damages.

But a wild card, called punitive damages, can change that result drastically. If a jury finds that the harm was caused maliciously or intentionally, it can punish the defendant, setting an amount of damages far above what's necessary to compensate the victim. There are no rules about what is a proper amount of punitive damages. The jury is expected to take into account the wealth of the defendant; the richer the defendant, the theory goes, the bigger the amount needed to make an impact. Appeals courts sometimes reduce punitive damages awards, but they still tend to be hefty—often, many times the amount of the other damages claimed.

Laws do not persuade just because they threaten.

—SENECA

There are several serious problems inherent in allowing punitive damages.

☞ If a business looks to have a high risk of incurring punitive damages awards, liability insurance becomes expensive—sometimes prohibitively so. So business owners simply stop risky activities. If you doubt this, try to remember the last time you saw a diving board at a public swimming pool.

☞ Huge judgments are often pinned on defendants arbitrarily. People guilty of truly bad behavior who have good lawyers may get off altogether, while people barely at fault can be ordered to pay millions. Obviously, the fact that jury awards are so unpredictable goes far to defeat the reason punitives are supposedly awarded—to punish and deter dishonest or dangerous conduct.

☞ Trial lawyers often convince juries to focus only on the needs of suffering victims and the wealth of the defendant, not on whether the defendant's conduct or product produced generally good results. For example, in the mid-1980s, manufacturers of the Sabin polio vaccine had to pay huge punitive damage awards to some people who suffered medical problems after taking the vaccine. This happened even though the U.S. government, after considering the risks, had recommended the vaccine because it provided far better immunity than others.

☞ The possibility of large punitive damages can slow down the introduction of new products. The price of innovation is that, inevitably, some mistakes will be made. Anyone hurt by these mistakes should be fairly and quickly compensated. At the same time, honest innovators should not be punished with huge punitive damage awards.

Trial lawyers argue that the mere possibility of punitive damages deters bad conduct—for example, if a manufacturer is tempted to sell a product it hasn't thoroughly tested or knows may be unsafe. But because punitive damages are awarded so arbitrarily, and a manufacturer or other business cannot predict when it may be at risk, all sorts of useful conduct is deterred while the real bad guys go right ahead.

If the punitive damages system works so poorly, why does it survive? Because it enriches many trial lawyers, who commonly receive 30% to 40% of jury awards. Lawyers milk the system in two ways. First, they convince juries to pin huge judgments on defendants rich enough (or with enough insurance) to pay. Second, they use the fear of a possible huge verdict to blackmail defendants into settling cases of dubious value. And to keep their honey pot full, trial lawyers' groups spend freely to lobby state legislatures and battle in appellate court to keep the system. Punitive damages would quickly disappear without lawyer-financed efforts.

Recently, in response to critics, some states have capped punitive damages at a certain amount, such as $250,000. Others have applied caps to certain types of cases, such as medical malpractice. While caps sound good, they work poorly in practice. Trial lawyers, fearing a loss of income, file more lawsuits to make up the difference.

What to Do

Punitive damages paid to the winner of a lawsuit should be eliminated. Far better to set up a more efficient system to make businesses liable to provide fast, fair compensation to anyone injured by substandard products or services.

If convincing evidence shows that a defendant's conduct was truly bad—fraudulent, or a willful violation of health and safety laws—the jury should have the power to recommend that state and local prosecutors press criminal charges or seek civil fines against the people responsible. And to ensure that the jury's recommendation is taken seriously, the prosecutor should be required either to follow it or explain in writing why not. The threat of jail time is a more effective deterrent than the risk of punitive damages, especially when corporate managers are the ones responsible for the actions. After all, punitive damages don't come out of their pockets—the corporation pays.

Here are some other reforms:

☞ *Standards for awarding puntive damages should be tightened.* Punitives should be an option for a jury only when bad conduct (gross negligence) results in extraordinary harm, such as death, serious physical injury or financial disaster. Toss out the rules that allow punitive damages whenever a defendant commits oppression, fraud or malice, even though the harm done is negligible.

☞ *Pay punitive damages to the state, not the plaintiff.* It's far better to have the money paid to the public treasury than to a victim, who has already been compensated for actual losses. Realizing this, a few states, including Florida, require that a substantial portion of a punitive damage award be paid to the state. Unfortunately, lawyer groups have had some success in getting these statutes tossed out.

☞ *The defendant's wealth should not be a factor.* Telling the jury how affluent the defendant is can produce huge punitive damage judgments . The idea is that to punish a wealthy person, you must make it hurt. Maybe so, but this approach has led to a worse evil: lawyers who shop for clients solely because there is a wealthy defendant. If we want to redistribute wealth, there are fairer ways to do it.

The Fickle Finger of Blame

A recent Alabama case is a good example of punitive damages run amok. In the case, Lemmie Ruffin, an insurance agent, sold group health and life insurance policies to cover several employees of Roosevelt City, Alabama. Their life insurance was placed with Pacific Mutual Life Insurance and the health insurance with Union Fidelity Life Insurance, but Ruffin told the city all the insurance was with Pacific Mutual. After a few months, Ruffin began pocketing the insurance premium money. The life and health policies were canceled, but the companies never notified the employees; they just notified Ruffin.

During this time, Cleopatra Haslip, who was covered by the health plan, became ill and incurred medical bills of $3,100. Because she had no insurance and couldn't pay them, the bill was turned over to a collection agency and her credit suffered.

Haslip and several other people in the failed insurance plan sued Ruffin and Pacific Mutual—which did not even sell health insurance—claiming fraud. A jury awarded Haslip her direct economic loss. And an extra $1 million in punitive damages.

{*Haslip v. Pacific Mutual Life Insurance Co.*, 499 U.S. 1 (1991).}

Allow People to Direct Their Own Medical Care

AT LEAST 10,000 AMERICANS ARE SUSPENDED, THROUGH MEDICAL MACHINATIONS, BETWEEN LIFE AND DEATH IN A PERSISTENT VEGETATIVE STATE. FOR THE GREAT MAJORITY, THIS IS CONTRARY TO THEIR WISHES. ANOTHER SEGMENT OF AMERICA—THE ELDERLY, THOSE WITH AIDS OR OTHER SERIOUS DISEASES—ARE DENIED THE MEDICAL CARE THAT WOULD MAKE THEIR LAST DAYS MORE BEARABLE OR MIGHT GIVE THEM HOPE FOR A CURE. THE LAW CRUELLY DENIES ALL OF THESE PEOPLE A SIMPLE WAY TO EXPRESS A BASIC RIGHT—THE RIGHT TO GET THE MEDICAL CARE THEY WANT.

Nearly 80% of all Americans die in a hospital or other care facility. And doctors who work there are generally charged with preserving a patient's life. This guiding proposition sometimes flies in the face of cost-efficiency and common sense—and most importantly, often contradicts what the patient would have wanted had he or she been able to express wishes. Doctors' egos are often at play, too. For many of them, keeping a patient alive with tubes, machines and chemicals is preferable to losing him or her through a natural death.

Of course, the reverse may also be true: A person may be provided with less extensive care than he or she would like. For example, a doctor may be unwilling to try experimental treatments or maintain long-term procedures on a patient he or she feels has slim chances of recovery. And a doctor may have far different views of what is proper treatment than the patient who slated to receive or be denied it.

The first legal wranglings over directing medical care were couched in terms of the Right To Die—cases that tested the bounds of what treatment can be administered in the face of a patient's desire to die naturally, free from artificial, life-prolonging machinery. Over time, the Right To Die took on a broader meaning, recognizing that patients' rights are paramount, and that some patients prefer that all possible treatment and procedures be used to treat them, even when that flies in the face of their doctor's asserted best medical judgment.

Waves of activism in the late 60s and early 70s led to catalytic consumer lobbying efforts for individual rights to direct healthcare. In 1976, California became the first state to pass a law allowing individuals to write healthcare directives— documents informing doctors of the specific kind of medical care they want provided, withheld or withdrawn. By the end of the 1980s, most states had followed suit.

In 1990, the U.S. Supreme Court, in *Cruzan v. Missouri Department of Health,* ruled that someone who wishes to direct his or her own medical treatment must make those wishes known by clear and convincing evidence. There are now two legally-recognized ways an individual can do this: by signing a durable power of attorney for healthcare or a living will.

There are serious disadvantages to both approaches. Few states expressly recognize durable powers of attorney for healthcare, limiting an attorney-in-fact's powers to supervising financial matters. And only about a dozen states allow people to appoint someone (called a proxy) to supervise living will wishes. Some states require a verified diagnosis of a terminal illness

> *For many, the thought of an ignoble end, steeped in decay, is abhorrent. A quiet, proud death, bodily integrity intact, is a matter of extreme consequence.*
>
> —U.S. SUPREME COURT JUSTICE WILLIAM BRENNAN

before either document becomes binding. Some apply only when a patient is diagnosed to be in a permanent coma. Some do not allow patients to refuse nutrition and hydration. And a number of states require that individuals use a specifically worded form to note directions for their medical care.

The result of all this legal and medical chaos is that experts now advise people to fill out both a durable power of attorney for healthcare and a living will. But it is difficult enough to get people to overcome psychological barriers and plan for death. Requiring two complicated and confusing forms surely impedes the effort.

What to Do

Those who want to put their healthcare wishes in writing should be able to do it by filling out one simple document, a Medical Treatment Statement. This document could take effect if an individual were diagnosed to have either a terminal condition or to be in a permanent coma. The Statement should be the same in all states and should:

☞ allow an individual to specify whatever treatment or medication should be administered or denied

☞ remain in effect until specifically revoked or changed

☞ be binding on treating physicians, but empower a named family member or friend to make sure all directions are followed, and

☞ be kept at a single, national office, so that physicians and hospitals could track down the information quickly and efficiently. This nonprofit, computerized system could easily be funded by requiring a slight charge to file or update a Statement. Most people would consider that money well spent for peace of mind for themselves and those close to them.

Individual doctors should be required to discuss the Medical Treatment Statement with patients, and hospitals should make them available as part of their admission procedure.

Defining the Documents

A durable power of attorney for healthcare is a document that allows a person to designate a trusted relative or friend as an attorney-in-fact to make medical care decisions on his or her behalf should the person become unable to do so. The advantage for a struggling or unaware patient is that another human being is authorized to supervise the care.

A living will is a document requiring a doctor to withdraw life-prolonging care, in certain circumstances, if a person later becomes unable to communicate those wishes. The advantage of a living will is that it contractually obligates the doctor to follow a patient's wishes for treatment or to find another doctor who will honor them.

> *A country man between two lawyers is like a fish between two cats.*
>
> —BENJAMIN FRANKLIN

Reform the Jury System

THE JURY SYSTEM IS INEFFICIENT—AND MISTREATS THOSE
IT RELIES UPON FOR HELP. JURORS MUST MAKE
EXCRUCIATINGLY DIFFICULT DECISIONS, BUT ARE GIVEN
ONLY GARBLED LEGALISTIC INSTRUCTIONS AND ARE
STRICTLY PROHIBITED FROM TAKING AN ACTIVE PART
IN TRIALS.

More Americans than ever are being called for jury duty.
Potential jurors spend most of their time in crowded holding
rooms. There they wait for hours, sometimes days, to find out
whether judges and attorneys will deign to call them into a
courtroom and assess their suitability as jurors. Many never get
called. Those who do often wish they hadn't been.

Many of those who are called for initial evaluation as jurors
are rejected, but only after attorneys and the judge publicly
subject them to intrusive and often irrelevant questioning: Have
you ever been raped? Have you ever stolen anything? Have you
ever been arrested for drunk driving?

And lawyers often settle cases moments before trial. Having
served as unwitting players in the bluffing game between
lawyers, many of whom never planned to go trial in the first
place, the jurors are told they are no longer needed after investing several days of their time and effort.

Those picked as jurors face a tough job. Some must evaluate
the graphic evidence of a violent crime, which may take a heavy
psychological toll. Others must listen to the laborious details of
a complicated civil lawsuit, which may try their patience. Many

jurors complain about lawyers' and judges' condescending attitudes. Others note that trials drag on days longer than necessary as attorneys pontificate and perform.

Another problem usually surfaces when the evidence is finally in: When they go to deliberate, jurors are often given instructions so laden with legal lingo that they're incomprehensible. If the jury pleads for help during deliberations, judges may refuse to give it, claiming fairness prevents them from explaining away the confusion. So after painstakingly listening to evidence, jurors often end up debating not the case before them, but the meaning of legal garble.

For doing what they feel is their civic responsibility, those summoned for jury duty are paid chump change—about $7 a day plus token mileage costs in most states. While this makes poor sense in criminal cases, it's an even stronger insult in civil matters, which are typically big dollar personal injury or business cases for which the lawyers charge huge fees.

What to Do

Jurors should be treated with the respect they deserve.

☞ Jurors should be paid a decent day's wage. For civil cases, juror pay should be charged to the litigating parties.

☞ Courts should expand the methods used to locate potential jurors. Most courts now use voter registration lists, taxing the patience of even the most civic-minded souls, who are called for jury duty after each election. Some courts now draw potential jurors from drivers' registration and state income taxation lists—a step in the right direction.

☞ Courts should adopt a one-day, one-trial system, now in place in a few courtrooms in Connecticut and Massachusetts.

> *Jury: a group of twelve men who, having lied to the judge about their hearing, health and business engagements, have failed to fool him.*
>
> —H.L. MENCKEN

Under that approach, a person who is called for a day of jury duty and is not assigned to a trial need not return. If chosen for a trial, however, the juror must serve as long as that trial lasts. More people are called for jury duty, making juries more representative. And it eliminates the idle waits jurors have when they are on call for several weeks.

☞ If jurors must be on call for longer than one day before being seated on a jury, they should not have to wait at the courthouse. Some courts now allow jurors to check in at the courthouse by telephone to see whether their services are required. But most require frequent checking, making it impossible to go to work or concentrate for long periods. One telephone check daily should be sufficient.

☞ Potential jurors should be sifted more efficiently. For example, many of the background questions that often disqualify a person as a juror, such as occupation or family make-up, could be answered in a simple questionnaire, so that those obviously disqualified could be dismissed. Only the more pointed questions on objectivity and bias would be posed and answered in a time-consuming court session.

☞ More courts should adopt the process pioneered in Wisconsin and now used in some other states, where jurors are encouraged to question the witnesses. Jurors submit written questions to the trial judge, who discusses each question with the attorneys in private. In the courtroom, the judge reads approved questions to the witnesses. The lawyers can clear up questions that are troubling the jury, and the jurors are more interested and attentive during the trial.

☞ Finally, all jury instructions should be clear and easy to understand. Accomplishing this should not be hard, since the same written instructions are used repeatedly. Each state should draw up uniform instructions which should pass muster by a Plain English Commission designated to review them.

Many Are Called

Percentage of adult Americans summoned for jury duty in 1990: 45
Percentage of those summoned in 1984: 35
Percentage of those summoned who actually serve as jurors: 17
Percentage who served as jurors two times or more: 7

Excuses, Excuses

Percentage of women excused from jury panels: 23
Percentage of men excused: 33

You Can Move, But You Cannot Hide

Percentage of people living in the western U.S. called for jury duty: 55
Percentage called in southern states: 51
Percentage called in eastern states: 43
Percentage called in midwest states: 34

Statistics from 1990 survey by Research & Forecasts, New York

Get a Consumer Voice
in the IRS

FEW THINGS FILL US WITH GREATER DREAD THAN
RECEIVING AN ENVELOPE BEARING THE RETURN ADDRESS
OF THE INTERNAL REVENUE SERVICE. THERE IS
INCREASING CAUSE FOR ALARM. THE POWERFUL IRS,
BEST-KNOWN FOR ITS DOGGEDNESS, IS INCREASINGLY
WRONG IN ITS TAX BILLS AND ASSESSMENTS. AND IT
REFUSES TO EXPLAIN ITSELF TO THE TAXPAYERS IT HOLDS
ACCOUNTABLE.

Nearly every year, the IRS claims it has finally simplified tax
forms, even dubbing one the EZ form. But it's taxing just to
read the instructions—such as this excerpt from the popular
Application for Extension of Time to File:

"The application for extension of time to file must
be submitted on or before the due date of the return or
the extended due date if you file for an Additional
extension of time after you have previously filed an
Automatic 4-month extension of time application. The
application should be submitted in sufficient time to
enable processing by the Department of Finance and
Revenue."

The IRS claims to provide help over a convenient Taxpayer
Assistance telephone hotline. But it is well-nigh impossible to
get through around tax time. Those who finally get past the

recording are often steered wrong. The IRS acknowledged recently that while the rate of accurate responses given on its hotline had increased, more than one out of four callers is misinformed.

In hunting down those who owe money, however, the 120,000-person IRS bureaucracy is more effective. The IRS is motivated by an estimated $80 to $100 billion each year that the taxpayers allegedly shortchange the government by not filing returns, underreporting income and overstating deductions. Another $90 billion remains due from those who admit they owe but cannot pay.

Doggedly going after the cheaters, the IRS notifies nearly 38 million individuals each year that they owe more in taxes and penalties. The top four failings, according to the IRS, are: math errors, returns filed late, misreported income, interest or dividends, and miscalculated quarterly payments.

But lest we all rest assured that the IRS is doing its job, heed the startlingly different picture revealed in a Gallup poll commissioned by *Money* magazine. Of those who contested tax due notices sent by the IRS, 45% reported the IRS claims were completely erroneous; an additional 24% said the agency was partially wrong. Of those who challenged the IRS, 53% wound up paying nothing, and another 17% paid a greatly reduced sum. Even the IRS, fessing up to its own mistakes, conservatively estimates that taxpayers saved more than $649 million in 1993 by not paying erroneously charged penalties.

Despite all the evidence that the IRS is so fuddled that it often goes after the wrong people for the wrong amounts, most people challenged by the IRS simply pay up and shut up. Those who fight back often wish they hadn't, as the IRS red tape, beginning with a series of progressively ominous letters, quickly ensnares them. The last letter arrives by certified mail and threatens that the federal government will clamp a lien on the taxpayer's property if the contested tax is not paid promptly.

Forty-seven percent of all the written responses to taxpayers are incorrect. How can we even contemplate prosecuting anybody?

—U.S. REP. CHRISTOPHER SHAYS

Compounding the fear created by the IRS's liberally applied scare tactics is a greater fear: Most taxpayers have no idea how to be sure that they are right. Tax laws are difficult to master, and they change yearly. Help from accountants and financial planners is often forbiddingly expensive. And even if the taxpayer is plainly right, proving it to the IRS typically requires a great deal of tenacity and a good many organized records and receipts. It may cost more money and energy to demonstrate that the IRS is wrong than to pay it money you do not owe.

What to Do

People are more likely to pay taxes when they understand what they owe and feel the collection process is fair. The IRS can meet these simple goals by:

☞ Making tax forms simple to fill out by rewriting them in clear language and providing concise instructions.

☞ Living accurate assistance to taxpayers who need more information. Taxpayer assistance phone lines should be adequately staffed by trained personnel so that taxpayers not only are able to reach help, but are given correct information when they do.

☞ Making it practical to file returns electronically. The IRS instituted the procedure a few years ago, but put many restrictions on how it could be done—requiring those who

> *If a lawyer and an IRS
> agent were both drowning,
> and you could save only
> one of them, would you go
> to lunch or read the paper?*

wished to file electronically to pay for a special IRS-approved transmitter, for example. And the efficiency of the system so far has been illusory. Most taxpayers paying electronically in 1993 waited as long to get their refunds as those who filed by mail. Transmitters should be made available for taxpayers at a number of convenient, public locales such as post offices. And as promised, returns filed electronically should be processed quickly.

☞ Creating an administrative appeal procedure to operate outside the IRS. The employees who would staff such a Taxpayer Rights office would have specific review authority in the following matters:

• recovery of-out-of pocket costs by taxpayers in fighting the IRS

• release of erroneous, premature or incorrectly filed liens

• recovery of civil damages for certain unauthorized collection actions

• abatement of interest for unreasonable IRS delay

• recovery of damages due to failure to release liens

• review of installment agreement disputes, and

• granting Taxpayer Assistance Orders that require the IRS to take certain actions such as promptly investigating a claim.

☞ Requiring the IRS to automatically grant installment agreements to taxpayers with clean payment records for the prior three years and who owe less than $10,000. This was partially adopted as policy by the IRS in 1993.

☞ Requiring the IRS to pay tax refund recipients the same rate of interest the IRS charges on late payments. It now pays one percentage point less.

A Hesitant Step in the Right Direction, Maybe

The IRS has set up the Problem Resolution Program (PRP)—a go-between service for taxpayers and the IRS to resolve problems. The 300 PRP offices nationwide handle taxpayer complaints from smoothing out discrepancies in state returns to delaying the time the IRS will seize property to satisfy back taxes.

But the program has two big drawbacks: Few people know it exists, and taxpayers must first run head-on into the IRS bureaucracy. PRP offices help only those who have received at least three complaint letters from the IRS or who have been treated rudely by IRS personnel. And a taxpayer must first have made at least two attempts to clear up the problem by calling the local tax office or the number listed on the IRS letter. PRP staffers do not help interpret tax laws; they assist only in cutting through the IRS's red tape. Call the toll-free number, (800) 829-1040, to find the nearest branch office.

End the Lawyer Monopoly: Bring Competition to the Law Business

LAWYERS, AS A GROUP, HAVE LONG ENJOYED A MONOPOLY IN SELLING LEGAL INFORMATION AND SERVICES. THE RESULT IS EXCESSIVE FEES FOR THOSE WHO CAN PAY—AND LITTLE OR NO LEGAL HELP FOR THOSE WHO CANNOT.

It is well-accepted that monopolies of all kinds cause large-scale inefficiencies, including higher prices and lower-quality goods and services. Because they are so destructive to our economy and freedom of choice, most are illegal. So too should be the lawyer cartel—an association of individual lawyers, law firms and state and local bar associations which together orchestrate both written and unwritten policies to fix prices and stamp out competition.

The lawyer cartel enforces its monopoly by making it a crime for anyone but lawyers to sell legal services. One way this is done is through "unauthorized practice of law" statutes passed by state legislatures at the behest of powerful lawyer members. A second is by having judges (who, after all, are lawyers) enforce court rules prohibiting non-lawyer practice.

The result is that most non-lawyers who try to provide help with legal paperwork at a reasonable price are scared out of business. If they persist, they may be fined or even sent to jail to

> *Lawyers earn a living by the sweat of browbeating others.*
>
> —JAMES GIBBONS HANEKER

drive home the message that competing with lawyers simply will not be tolerated.

Laws prohibiting non-lawyers from "practicing law" never define what practicing law consists of, except to say that it's what lawyers do or are trained to do. The absence of any meaningful legal standard allows judges to use their own seat-of-the-pants opinions to decide whether non-lawyers on trial should be punished for infringing on the legal profession's turf. Most judges rule that any non-lawyer who sells even the most basic consumer information about debts, divorce or even traffic tickets is guilty of a criminal offense.

Appallingly, judges enforce these rules even when:

☞ People obviously can't afford lawyers.

☞ There are no lawyers available.

☞ The advice or information given by non-lawyers is accurate and up-to-date.

The lawyer cartel's persistent, often blatant efforts to prevent honest competition in the business of delivering legal services amount to a classic conspiracy to limit competition and fix prices. Doesn't that violate America's anti-monopoly laws? Yes, but it makes no difference. The legal profession simply isn't forced to obey the law. The reason, of course, is that enforcement must come from prosecutors and judges who, as lawyers themselves, were trained to believe that only lawyers should sell legal information. (See Proposal #40, Appoint Non-Lawyers as Judges, for a discussion of how this pro-lawyer bias could be reduced if non-lawyers served as judges.)

The lawyer cartel is also firmly in the driver's seat when it comes to a citizen's right to hire a non-lawyer paralegal as a

courtroom advocate. Judges, asserting their independent constitutional authority ("inherent powers," in lawyer jargon) to
regulate who appears before them as advocates, arrogantly ban
all paralegals. They are deemed incompetent, as a group; no
effort is made to assess the competence of individual paralegals.
And judges continue to do this even though many privately
agree with Warren Burger, former Chief Justice of the U.S.
Supreme Court, who opined that a substantial percentage of trial
lawyers themselves are incompetent.

Disgusting as it is for lawyers to abuse the legal system by
shutting down and jailing their competitors, the cartel's real
victims are the millions of Americans who are priced out of the
legal system as a result. Eighty percent of the people in this
country can't afford basic legal services, according to Attorney
General Janet Reno. Even the American Bar Association con-
cedes that as many as 100 million Americans cannot afford
fundamental legal help. Yet the ABA and its affiliate state bar
associations refuse to seriously entertain the obvious solution:
allow qualified non-lawyers to deliver routine legal services at an
affordable price.

Despite their claims to the contrary, lawyers put self-interest
ahead of public interest. Just listen to Thomas R. Curtin,
president of the New Jersey State Bar Association. In a 1993
letter to all state bar presidents, he warned against an ABA
commission that was discussing the idea of non-lawyers providing "services that have traditionally been offered only by lawyers." Such a move would have

> "serious implications for the bar, particularly for solo
> practitioners and small firms... These are difficult times
> economically for the profession in New Jersey and, I am
> sure, in many other places as well. I am concerned that
> the Commission is engaged in an effort that is directly
> contrary to the interests of lawyers."

> *While competition cannot be created by statutory enactment, it can in large measure be revived by changing the laws and forbidding the practices that killed it.*
>
> —WOODROW WILSON

What to Do

Laws and court rules that prohibit practicing law without a license should be repealed. Non-lawyers should be free to provide basic legal services, including preparing the paperwork for divorces, bankruptcies, probates and most other routine uncontested actions.

In most states, repeal of these laws must come from state legislatures, most of which are heavily influenced by lawyers. But in a few states, where measures with enough grassroots support can be put right on the ballot, interested consumers could push for these changes directly.

This new deregulated system would benefit lawyers as well as consumers. Lawyers would quickly shift from low-skill legal tasks, such as handling uncontested probates, guardianships or divorces, to areas involving more technical knowledge, much as doctors have turned the task of taking peoples' temperature and blood pressure and running diagnostic machines over to others. Most would make a better living doing more interesting work, and the profession as a whole would no longer be seen by the public as a price-gouging monopoly.

To imagine how this system would work, consider the tax preparation field today. A person who wants help filling out a tax return or advice about tax strategy has lots of choices. He or she can go to a low-cost tax preparation center (a large outfit like H & R Block or an individual), an enrolled agent, a certified public accountant or a tax lawyer. Understanding that prices, types of service and customer recourse in case of difficulty vary

considerably, it's up to each consumer to choose. In short, as long as the non-lawyer tax preparer, accountant or lawyer is honest about his or her credentials, the marketplace takes care of the rest.

In this deregulated environment, the public should be protected from dishonest or incompetent providers. To this end, everyone who provides legal services—lawyers and non-lawyers alike—should be required to register with a state agency and prominently display their educational qualifications and experience. In the future, should we learn that more regulation is necessary, it may be reasonable to also require providers of certain types of legal services to pass a skills-based examination.

Q: How many lawyers can you place on the head of a pin?

A: Ten, if you make them stand on their heads

The Law Store

Deregulating the legal services business would allow law stores, on the order of H & R Block tax preparation offices, to open on every corner.

The typical law store, staffed by both lawyers and non-lawyers, would offer consumers a range of legal services. It would sell self-help law books, software and audio and videotapes. It would also provide low-cost access to a user-friendly computer connected to a legal database so that people could look up information.

Typists would charge by the page for completing legal documents prepared by customers using self-help law materials. Non-lawyers trained in specific legal subject areas, such as family law or bankruptcy, would provide information and prepare forms for customers who were willing to pay higher fees for it and even represent people before administrative hearings and in routine court actions. Attorneys would be available to offer legal diagnoses and consultations on especially knotty issues and representation in more complicated contested court proceedings. (See Proposal #42, Free Lawyers to Help Self-Helpers: 'Unbundle' Legal Services, for more on how legal services can be efficiently provided using new, affordable techniques.)

Restrict Lawyers' Licenses

A LICENSE TO PRACTICE LAW IS NO GUARANTEE OF LEGAL
KNOWLEDGE, SKILL OR EXPERIENCE. INCOMPETENT
LAWYERS REGULARLY MISLEAD AND DEFRAUD CLIENTS WHO
RELY ON THE PROMISE OF EXPERTISE THAT THE LAWYER
LABEL BRINGS.

People who go to lawyers have the right to expect what they
pay for: competent legal advice. But as many clients discover, a
license to practice law is no promise of knowledge of a particular
legal area. Even worse, some clients never discover that they got
faulty advice or representation and that shoddy lawyering may
have cost them important rights—and their savings.

According to state bar associations (the lawyers' groups who
hand out law licenses), aspiring lawyers undergo rigorous
training and pass a tough exam before being loosed on the
public. Only these specially-trained people, according to the bar,
can cope with the complexities of our legal system.

In fact, most law schools teach little about how the law
actually works or about how to deal with clients or courts.
Instead, schools concentrate on the decisions of appeals courts
and legal history and theory. That bears little relation to why
most people hire lawyers. People need lawyers who can consult
and interpret the relevant laws, advise on possible courses of
action and prepare the right paperwork.

The bar exam is even more out of touch. The day-to-day
skills lawyers are commonly believed to possess—research,
writing, counseling clients, dealing with courts, mastering a

wide variety of basic legal concepts—are not tested. Fledgling lawyers are expected to pick up these skills after they have their licenses, giving a disturbing meaning to the expression "practicing law."

Once they hurdle the bar exam, lawyers are never tested again. Some states require lawyers to take continuing education classes, but these requirements are minimal. In some states, lawyers may even get credit for watching videotapes on how to build their own self-esteem.

But what is most outrageous about licenses to practice law is their breadth. They give lawyers the right to take on any kind of case, from divorce to murder to zoning. Any lawyer is free to list any number of alleged specialties in a yellow pages ad or on a business card, even if he or she has no experience in that area of law.

What to Do

Lawyers' licenses should be limited to certain subject areas—for example, family law, criminal law, tax or probate. A separate exam should be given for each specialty. That way, an exam could test the skills and knowledge needed by a lawyer who wants to represent clients in a particular legal subject area.

> *Lawyer: An individual whose principal role is to protect his clients from others of his profession.*

Like pilots who must have a license for each type of aircraft they want to fly, law school graduates could take as many of the exams and amass as many of the limited licenses as they wanted. People hiring a lawyer would then have a much better idea of what kind of expertise they were getting.

Several other reforms would complement this fundamental change in lawyer licensing:

☞ Law schools should offer more practical courses, including trial practice, client counseling and other subjects that directly pertain to law practice.

☞ Before new lawyers are licensed and turned out into the community, they should be required to serve a one-year apprenticeship in a specialty they have chosen. Such a program should not merely supply cheap labor for law firms. It must require structured supervision from a lawyer who has a license in the specialty and experience in specific, practical areas of the field. After the apprenticeship period, the new lawyer would be eligible to take the exam to get a license in that specialty.

☞ Testing on substantive law and procedure should continue as long as a lawyer practices. As it is, people are periodically re-tested before renewing their driver's licenses, but a lawyer's license is good for life. It is taken away only if the worst misconduct can be proven—a rare event.

Make Traffic Court Fair

PEOPLE WHO WANT TO FIGHT AN UNFAIR TRAFFIC TICKET COMMONLY ARE KEPT IGNORANT OF THEIR RIGHTS AND MUST OVERCOME INSULTING AND UNNECESSARY BUREAUCRATIC OBSTACLES. WHEN THEY FINALLY GET TO COURT, THEY ARE TYPICALLY PRESUMED TO BE LYING AND ARE ALMOST AUTOMATICALLY FOUND GUILTY.

Going to traffic court could be a valuable lesson in civics—a chance to have the satisfaction of getting one's day in court before an impartial judge. Instead, people encounter a bureaucratic maze designed to discourage them from fighting their tickets. Those who persist too often find their cases heard in a kangaroo court atmosphere, in which they're guilty until they prove themselves innocent.

Typically, someone who receives a traffic citation must trek to the courthouse and wait in a long line to get an appointment. Weeks or even months later, the traffic offender must again journey to court—only to say the words "not guilty" at an arraignment. Then the judge sets a trial date a few more weeks or months away. To add further insult to the inconvenience, in many places, a citizen must pay the fine (post bail) before the trial date.

When the trial day finally arrives, things usually get worse—especially for a busy person who has had to take off from work. For starters, there is likely to be a long wait. When the case is finally called, the judge will probably accept the officer's statement of what happened without question—while barely

> *A lawyer's job is secure—who would build a robot to do nothing?*

listening to any other version. In some courts, judges even refuse to look at pictures or diagrams offered by defendants, or listen to their legal arguments if they aren't represented by lawyers. In short, no matter how strong a case, there is an overwhelming likelihood that someone accused of a traffic violation will be found guilty.

In the age of "no new taxes," politicians desperate to balance the books have lost sight of the purpose of traffic laws—to discourage unsafe driving—and view them instead as a way to bring in money. Because many people wisely conclude that it's easier to pay a fine than to put in time standing in line on three different days just to get an unfair trial, the government has a sure moneymaker by keeping things the way they are.

If this all sounds like a conspiracy, there's good reason. To understand it, you need only look at how the large revenues generated by traffic court fines are divvied up. A typical state might operate like this: First, there's a "penalty assessment" over and above the amount of the ticket; that goes for courthouse and jail construction. Then, the city whose officer gave the ticket gets a cut. Much of this money, sometimes a fixed percentage, goes directly to the police department's budget. Next, the courts get a percentage. In some places, traffic court revenues are used to pay judges or fund pension plans.

It's not only greed that causes traffic court judges to side with police officers in court: The judges must run for re-election regularly. To keep their jobs, they usually want the influential support of the local police officers' association. One good way to get this support is to side with police officers in traffic cases most of the time.

What to Do

Traffic court should treat people fairly and efficiently at the same time that it deters unsafe driving. Here's how:

☞ Sever the connection between traffic fines and courthouse and police funding. A good place to put the money would be to fund traffic safety programs.

☞ Include basic instructions on how people can assert their rights to a fair hearing on an information sheet handed out with the ticket. Back this up with a courthouse voice mail system which routes information requests to recorded messages or, if necessary, someone who can answer questions.

☞ Allow people to enter not guilty pleas and arrange court appearances by mail or phone.

☞ Schedule court appearances at convenient hours, including Saturdays and evenings.

☞ Train and retrain commissioners and judges who hear traffic court cases to scrupulously try to find the truth, and not just rely on the police officer's story.

☞ Take politics out of traffic court. Cases should be heard by appointed commissioners who can judge on the merits, not with half their attention on the next election.

Tell the truth and run.

—YUGOSLAV PROBERB

Reform the Child Support System

ABOUT 25% OF AMERICAN CHILDREN NOW LIVE IN
POVERTY. MANY OF THEM ARE IN FAMILIES HEADED BY
SINGLE PARENTS, DEPENDENT UPON SUPPORT FROM THE
OTHER PARENT. BUT, TOO OFTEN, COURT-ORDERED
SUPPORT ISN'T PAID—A PROBLEM MADE WORSE BY
INEFFICIENT AND COSTLY COLLECTION BUREAUCRACIES
OPERATED BY THE STATES.

When parents split up, one of them—most often the
mother—gets physical custody of the children. The other parent
becomes obligated to pay child support. In some instances, the
support payments are enough, when added to the other income,
to provide the children with a decent life. But more often, the
actual contributions are far too little.

Whether adequate child support is paid depends on both the
efficiency of the enforcement effort and the responsible parent's
health, attitude, employment and other financial obligations,
including the need to support a second family. Severe restrictions on visitation rights, whether justified or not, often cause a
parent to hold back support payments.

A good many parents, despite any number of court orders
and stringent enforcement efforts, will not pay any support for
their children. They are unemployed, chronic drug and alcohol
abusers or impossible to track down. Under the current legal

system, their children, innocent victims of circumstance, get nothing.

What to Do

The current system of enforcing support obligations should be scrapped, and replaced with a new federal system for collecting and distributing child support. The new system should be guided by two simple principles. First, all children, regardless of their parents' income, should receive at least enough support to keep them out of poverty. Second, all parents should contribute to their children's support. Money to pay for supplementary support for children whose parents can't provide the minimum acceptable amount could come from the billions of dollars made available by a tough and efficient new collection system.

The new collection system should look like this:

☞ All child support awards set by local courts would conform to national minimum needs standards.

☞ All support orders would be registered with the Internal Revenue Service, which would collect the payments—either directly from paychecks or through quarterly estimated child support contribution returns—and deposit them into a Children's Support Fund.

☞ Random audits focusing on the self-employed and others who receive income from sources other than conventional employment would bring in millions of dollars that currently isn't collected.

☞ The inefficient state-run child support collection

> *So long as little children are allowed to suffer, there is no true love in the world.*
>
> —ISADORA DUNCAN

*Between grand theft and a
legal fee,
There only stands a
law degree.*

bureaucracies would be closed down, and the state and federal money slated each year to fund them would go into the Children's Support Fund.

The new disbursement system should look like this:

☞ Child support checks would be mailed monthly, as Social Security checks are now.

☞ Children would receive all money contributed to the Support Fund by their parents.

☞ If a child's parent contributed less than the federal minimum needs standard, the child would receive a supplemental amount from the Support Fund large enough to reach that standard.

☞ If a paying parent became unable to contribute because of a bona fide job loss or injury, he could describe the circumstances on a form to be submitted under oath to the IRS. The form would later be checked against the employer's payroll records. In the meantime, the parent's contribution would be adjusted downwards for a period not to exceed three months in any one calendar year. If a longer period were required, he could go back to court—in an informal proceeding without lawyers—to ask for an extension.

*What's the difference
between a poisonous snake
and a lawyer?*

*You can make a pet out of
the snake.*

Compensate Medical Malpractice Victims

Victims of medical malpractice are injured twice: first by faulty medicine, then by a famously slow legal system that requires them to prove who caused their injuries. And because a few who win get unrealistically high awards, health insurance costs rise for everyone, and doctors are scared into practicing defensive medicine.

Fewer than 5% of the people injured while under medical care receive any compensation. To win a medical malpractice lawsuit, a victim must prove who caused the injury—an extremely difficult task given the complexities of modern medicine and the common reaction of doctors, which is to cover up their mistakes.

A recent study of 33,000 New York hospital patients showed that nearly 1,400 of them suffered harm beyond the expected risks of their treatment—injuries that totaled $895 million in medical bills and lost wages. But only one in four could trace the injury to a specific person's careless act.

Indeed, primarily because patients have a difficult time proving who caused their injuries, the majority of those who sue for malpractice do not fare well; only 20% win. And they wait an average of seven years before getting a penny. Much of the amount awarded by a jury—commonly, 30 to 40%—goes to pay the lawyers.

But even though most malpractice victims are shortchanged, the healthcare system is choking on the cost of these lawsuits. Annual malpractice insurance premiums have shot up, some into the six-figure range. This contributes to the big medical bills that in turn make health insurance unaffordable for millions.

Lawyers contend that the medical profession needs the threat of huge jury awards as an incentive to police itself. Yet the opposite may be true: Doctors who are justifiably afraid of lawsuits may cover up for each other when mistakes are made.

Doctors' fears of malpractice awards also results in bad medical care. Both overtesting and overtreating are standard methods of beating malpractice suits. The result: thousands of unneeded surgeries are performed each year in the U.S., and expensive technology is regularly misused—CAT scans to diagnose simple headaches, for example.

Paradoxically, some doctors also try to avoid liability by undertreating. Because new procedures carry a higher risk of harm and of second-guessing later, doctors often stick to conventional treatments, even in terminal cases, for fear of lawsuits alleging that the advanced treatment hastened the patient's death.

What to Do

We should adopt a no-fault method to compensate all patients injured while under medical care. The system would:

☞ quickly compensate all who have suffered harm as a result of medical treatment, regardless of how it occurred

☞ give doctors incentives to root out and expose the causes of medical error

☞base a victim's economic recovery on actual economic loss—medical costs, loss of income and disability—plus, where there is long-term or permanent disability, a reasonable amount for lost quality of life, and

☞ handle compensation through a state-run Injured Patients Board, which could track information with a beefed-up Medical Board that monitors doctors.

A no-fault insurance system that would compensate all medical malpractice victims for economic loss would be expensive to administer. But it would cost no more than doctors and hospitals now spend on inflated malpractice insurance premiums each year. Real savings would also result from the substantial reduction of overtreatment and unnecessary operations.

The Insurance Industry: A Partner in the Crime

The insurance industry is as much to blame for the current crisis as is the legal system. While crying poor for the last 15 years and blaming it on vast jury awards and a lawsuit-happy society, insurers have made big bucks. Consider these facts recently uncovered by the General Accounting Office:

☞ Only state agencies oversee the industry; it is exempt from both antitrust laws and the Federal Trade Commission.

☞ Half of all malpractice claims are unsettled five years after they have been claimed.

☞ The insurance industry routinely underreports its rate of return on investments and overstates inflation when requesting rate hikes. And it gets them.

☞ Half of all personal bankruptcies in the U.S. in a given year are the result of unexpected illness.

Free Small Businesses From the Securities Laws

NEW CORPORATIONS AND EXISTING ONES SEARCHING FOR INVESTORS ARE BEING STRANGLED IN A SNARL OF SECURITIES LAWS, REGULATIONS AND RED TAPE. THEY MUST COMPLETE MOUNTAINS OF COMPLICATED LEGAL AND FINANCIAL DISCLOSURE PAPERWORK, MOST OF WHICH DOES LITTLE TO PROTECT INVESTORS FROM UNSCRUPULOUS PROMOTERS. WHAT IT DOES IS DIVERT MONEY TO LAWYERS AND ACCOUNTANTS.

America depends on small, privately-held businesses to provide innovative goods and services and create new jobs. This benefit of more jobs is particularly significant in today's volatile economy, when automation and overseas plants are replacing more and more domestic manufacturing jobs, and many pub-licly-held corporations are merging and eliminating middle management positions.

Of course, finding people willing to invest in the uncertain prospects of new business can be difficult. Unfortunately, federal and state securities laws make it even tougher, requiring a complicated and costly ritual of paperwork and procedures before outside investment capital can be solicited. For example, you cannot simply call potential investors—even friends or relatives—to see if they are interested in putting money in your small corporation. First you must comply with the federal securities laws and the securities statutes of your state and the home state of each person contacted.

Soliciting funds from the public is particularly burdensome. It involves filing a stock offering registration with federal and state agencies, preparing disclosure documents and stock offering materials for potential investors, and preparing complicated financial statements. The price tag in accounting and legal fees to generate this paperwork can easily be tens of thousands of dollars.

If you limit your stock offering to a close circle of business associates, friends and relatives or if you seek to raise only a modest amount of money, you may be able to qualify for federal and state exemptions from a full registration of your stock offering.

Although this will save you some time and money and avoid some of the pitfalls of a public offering, you still face a difficult and costly task. These exemptions are highly technical, vary significantly in their requirements, and often require preparing disclosure documents and filing notification forms with state and federal agencies.

The result for most small businesses, whether they qualify for a securities exemption or not, is a series of consultations with a lawyer and an accountant before accepting any funds from outsiders—and inevitably, a hefty bill for services rendered.

It is difficult to justify subjecting small businesses to this sort of procedural overkill. After all, the most unsophisticated consumer can invest a lifetime's savings in a speculative stock issue or commodities investment in the course of a telephone conversation with a stockbroker. The law requires no individual formalities or disclosures.

And the special securities disclosure paperwork rarely leads to any discoveries or second thoughts by prospective investors.

The legal language in these forms is so technical that it is unintelligible to the average investor. And, of course, financial

> *Perfect freedom is as necessary to the health and vigor of commerce, as it is to the health and vigor of citizenship.*
>
> —PATRICK HENRY

disclosure data can easily be exaggerated by unscrupulous entrepreneurs to overstate the financial prospects of any venture.

Most states and the federal government have special rules that apply to corporate "promoters"— people who help obtain money, property, personnel and whatever else it takes to get a new business up and running. The laws require promoters to disclose facts to all investors in all securities transactions and fill out reams of additional legalese-laden forms. These formalities add nothing but frustration to the small business startup. They have no practical legal effect.

What to Do

Small business owners should be free to raise startup or expansion money privately from friends, family and others without complicated disclosure procedures or securities filings. The hundreds of nitpicky federal and state regulations should be replaced by one simple one. It should exempt all securities transactions involving private companies and individual investors. As long as the investment funds are put to the uses for which they were solicited, investors should be able to assume the risks of the investment by signing a plain statement to this effect on a standard disclosure form.

This new disclosure form would be used to register the sales of the securities under this exemption and would be filed with a central agency, such as the federal Securities Exchange Commission. The exemption form should be simple and comprehensible. No one should need an accountant or lawyer to make sense of it. An example of such a statement is shown below.

Investors could still be protected against dishonest business promoters by the federal and state securities laws that deal specifically with misrepresentation and fraud.

A PRIVATE INVESTOR
DISCLOSURE STATEMENT

I UNDERSTAND THAT THIS IS AN UNCERTAIN AND RISKY INVESTMENT. DESPITE ANY ASSUR-ANCES OR EXPECTATIONS TO THE CONTRARY, I UNDERSTAND THAT I MAY NOT RECEIVE A RE-TURN ON THIS INVESTMENT AND MAY, IN FACT, LOSE ALL OF THE FUNDS INVESTED. I UNDER-STAND AND ASSUME THESE RISKS.

What do you get when you cross a lawyer with a demon from hell?

Another lawyer.

Protect Consumers From Unscrupulous, Overcharging and Incompetent Lawyers

WHEN LAWYERS MISHANDLE A CASE, ABANDON A CLIENT, OVERCHARGE OR STEAL A CLIENT'S MONEY, THE CLIENT IS ALMOST ALWAYS OUT OF LUCK. THERE'S JUST NOWHERE TO TURN FOR ANY HOPE OF REAL REDRESS. THOSE WHO COMPLAIN TO AUTHORITIES ARE RELEGATED TO A LAWYER-RUN DISCIPLINE SYSTEM DESIGNED TO PROTECT THE PROFESSION, NOT THE PUBLIC.

Each year, more clients file complaints against their lawyers with state bar associations or lawyer-controlled state regulatory agencies. Over 90% are dismissed without any investigation.

A glance at the system explains why. At bottom, these agencies are lawyers' trade groups, reluctant to discipline their own members. Even when a lawyer is accused of violating the law or stealing, clients are typically left unsatisfied, uncompensated and without the time or energy to fix the resulting legal problem.

But institutionalized bias is only part of the problem. Although many consumers find it hard to believe, these agencies simply aren't set up to help clients. At the most, they toss out a few bad apples who have become an embarrassment to the

Court: A room wherein are commonly found large numbers of thieves, rapists, muggers, arsonists, perverts, degenerates and lawyers.

profession. So even though an unscrupulous lawyer may be suspended from practice or disbarred, the client gets nothing.

The most common consumer complaint about lawyers is fee-gouging. In most states, these grievances are referred to panels of local lawyers in private practice, who probably know the lawyer accused of overbilling. The results are as predictable as would be trying a chicken in court where the judge is a fox. After cursory consideration, the panel usually concludes that the lawyer's bill is reasonable and that the client should do the decent thing and write a check.

Another widespread complaint from clients is that their lawyers are incompetent. But again, almost unbelievably, lawyer incompetence—even repeated and serious incompetence—is almost never considered a reason to discipline lawyers. Even when a lawyer flagrantly mishandles a case, attorney discipline officials routinely dismiss the unhappy client's complaint and suggest suing for malpractice. That's scant comfort, since those who have been burned by lawyer stupidity find it hard to get a second lawyer to take the case, and even if they do, harder still to prevail. (And because lawyers know they'll rarely have to pay for misdeeds, the malpractice system provides little incentive to do a decent job in the future.)

In the unlikely event a discipline proceeding is initiated against a lawyer, only a minuscule number of complaints lead to a substantial punishment. In fact, the most common "penalty" amounts to little more than the regulatory agency dismissing the case in exchange for which the lawyer promises not to be bad in the future.

If a lawyer is found guilty of misappropriation of funds, client abandonment or another serious misdeed, punishment is usually a slap on the wrist. Most often, the lawyer receives only a private reprimand or brief suspension from practice. Even in the rare instances when a lawyer is "permanently" suspended or disbarred, the lawyer can often successfully lobby to be readmitted to practice within a few years.

A big reason why lawyers get away with this cover-up of professional incompetence and malpractice is that lawyer disciplinary proceedings are almost always conducted by other lawyers in secret. In many states, not even the person who files the complaint knows what's going on. For example, in New Jersey, all disciplinary complaints are handled by volunteer local lawyers, who conduct their hearings in secret. It takes four years to produce an attorney suspension, five years for a disbarment.

The lawyer disciplinary system fails another crucial responsibility because it doesn't warn the public about poor lawyers. In most states, the fact that a complaint—or two dozen complaints—have been filed against a lawyer is not made public. In New Jersey, even a complaint containing information so damaging that it eventually leads to a lawyer being disbarred is kept secret during the five-year period it takes to pull the offending lawyer's license.

In answer to a mounting public outcry against crooked, incompetent and overcharging lawyers, a few lawyers have begun to advocate reform. In 1989, an American Bar Association commission (known as the McKay Commission) found that self-policing by the organized bar is a poor system. It detailed 22 recommendations to make lawyer discipline more accountable to the public, including having non-lawyers as disciplinary judges, holding disciplinary proceedings in public, and most important, freeing the proceedings from control of the organized bar. The McKay commission recommendations, published in a report called "Lawyer Regulations for a New Century," have been for the most part ignored.

One partial exception is California, where the number of lawyers disciplined immediately jumped 44% when the state bar upped its discipline budget 75%, adding a full-time court to hear discipline complaints. (Ever since, California lawyers have complained bitterly about the increase in state bar dues to pay for prosecuting their own, and many have lobbied to gut the system.) Another is Oregon, where client complaints against lawyers are public from the day they are filed.

Unfortunately, most reform efforts target lawyers who steal from clients or commit other crimes. But what is really needed is a system that weeds out incompetent lawyers and quickly compensates their victims. Don't count on this happening anytime soon. Lawyers have resisted all efforts to monitor the quality of service they provide through peer review procedures, such as those routinely used in the medical profession.

What to Do

The current system excludes consumers and hands lawyers the impossible task of policing themselves. It should be replaced by a fair, fast, public and accessible system that can resolve a wide range of consumer complaints against lawyers. Some of the ideas that follow were inspired by Deborah M. Chalfie's excellent article, "Dumping Discipline: A Consumer Protection Model for Regulating Lawyers," 4 Loyola Consumer Law Rptr. 4 (1991).

Lawyer discipline should be put in the hands of independent state regulatory agencies composed primarily of non-lawyers. These consumer-controlled agencies should have broad power to investigate lawyer conduct and competence, not just wait for consumers to complain.

> Lawyer: One who protects us against robbers by taking away the temptation.
>
> —H.L. MENKEN

When a member of the public does file a complaint, it should be evaluated as are other consumer problems, such as auto or home repair rip-offs. The agency should not only punish wrongdoing lawyers but also compensate victimized clients. Here are some specifics:

☞ A record of all complaints filed against lawyers, including those for incompetence, dishonesty or problems with drugs and alcohol, should be easily available to the public as soon as they are filed.

☞ The results of all official disciplinary investigations should be made public. No more private reprimands.

☞ Lawyers' trust accounts, which hold clients' money, should be regularly and independently audited. Lawyers who steal a client's money should be forever prevented from practicing law and prosecuted like other thieves.

☞ Serious charges that a lawyer has provided incompetent service should be quickly investigated by regulatory agencies. When incompetence is a pattern or causes substantial harm, the lawyer should be promptly suspended. Before being allowed to practice again, the lawyer should be required to compensate the victimized client and pass a tough proficiency exam.

☞ Clients should be compensated for losses they suffer from incompetent lawyering, including money for out-of-pocket losses. If the lawyer who causes the problem can't pay, compensation should be provided through a state fund, with the money raised by taxing all practicing lawyers.

Legal Malpractice: A Remedy Without Reason

State regulatory agencies tell clients who complain of lawyer incompetence to file a malpractice lawsuit. But those who do usually find that the effort wasn't worth it, as evidenced by some alarming statistics released by the American Bar Association:

☞ Fewer than 30% of all malpractice complaints filed against lawyers between 1983 and 1985 led to lawsuits.

☞ Clients received no compensation in more than 63% of malpractice lawsuits.

☞ Extremely few clients won more than $1,000.

☞ Clients who don't settle out of court win only 1.2% of the time.

One reason why malpractice cases are so hard to win is that the client must not only show that the lawyer screwed up, but also that the client would have prevailed in the underlying lawsuit. This often impossible legal standard should be changed. When serious acts of malpractice are proven, the victimized client should win unless the lawyer can prove that the malpractice didn't affect the outcome of the case.

Mediate Neighborhood Disputes

THE CLAIMS THAT MANY NEIGHBORS ARE LESS THAN NEIGHBORLY RUN THE GAMUT: THEY ARE LOUD. THEY REFUSE TO PITCH IN TO REPAIR THE FENCE ON THE LOT LINE. THEIR KIDS ARE DANGEROUS LITTLE MONSTERS WHO MENACE OTHERS. THE LEGAL SYSTEM—EXPENSIVE, SLOW AND ADVERSARIAL—IS ILL-EQUIPPED TO RESOLVE THESE DISPUTES.

Most neighbor disputes, no matter how acrimonious, are defined by the legal system as "not legal"—a definition that conveniently allows them to be ignored. Too often, the result is that these disputes fester, dividing the neighborhood and sometimes even ending in violence. Law enforcement and social agencies must cope as best they can with the unhappy result.

Treating a human problem as a police problem is a mistake. Providing arguing neighbors with a chance to resolve their disputes out of court, through mediation, is a far better alternative. In mediation, people who have a dispute meet with a trained mediator and negotiate a compromise both are willing to live with. It's a fair, fast, inexpensive and satisfying way to get to the bottom of disputes.

The mediator acts both as a skilled moderator, making sure each side gets a chance to speak up, and as a problem solver, helping both to define the dispute and arrive at an acceptable

> *Discourage litigation.*
> *Persuade your neighbors to*
> *compromise whenever you can.*
> *Point out to them how the*
> *nominal winner is often a*
> *real loser—in fees, expenses*
> *and waste of time.*
>
> —ABRAHAM LINCOLN

solution. There are no complicated procedural rules, no transcript, no court schedules, no judges, no lawyers. If the neighbors need more time to hammer out a resolution, they can schedule more meetings. Not only is their settlement apt to be more pleasing than one dictated by the court system, but they can reach it in private. Contrast this approach to the expense and paranoia that inevitably accompanies the lawyer-controlled dog and pony show that masquerades as our trial court system.

Mediation is an especially good way to resolve many neighborhood disputes because it not only prevents the current dispute from escalating, but provides a framework for future cooperation. Neighbors, after all, have a stake in establishing a civil long-term relationship.

The number of community mediation programs is burgeoning. A decade ago, there were fewer than 100 programs nationwide; by 1994, there were over 400 programs, in nearly every state. And they get results. Mediation services report a settlement rate of between 80 and 90% of all cases. (If mediation fails, both sides are free to file a lawsuit.)

Despite this rapid growth, most Americans still have no access to a community-based mediation program. Some functioning programs exist are poorly publicized. In some places, the system has been too heavily infiltrated by lawyers, who tend to hinder rather than help by pitting the two sides against one another and turning negotiations into arguments.

What to Do

Mediation must be embraced as a preferred method for settling neighborhood disputes. Local community-based programs should offer free or reasonably-priced mediation.

Strong links should be maintained with small claims courts. Before neighbor disputes go to court, small claims court staff should evaluate them with the idea of diverting as many as possible to mediation. It can work. In Maine, where all contested small claims court cases are now referred to a mediator, over half are settled.

Mandatory training for mediators should emphasize the skills necessary to help disputants reach a compromise. Judges and lawyers schooled in the adversarial dispute resolution techniques of the courtroom need rigorous screening and retraining before becoming mediators.

Finally, mediated solutions arrived at by the parties themselves should be as binding as any court judgment, eliminating the need to take the whole dispute to court if one party later backs out of the agreement.

Resources

To see whether free or low-cost neighborhood mediation is available in your community, contact the small claims clerk at the courthouse, the county law librarian or the police department. If you live in a planned unit development or subdivision, your homeowners' association may offer mediation services to members.

To find a mediation program, you can also contact:
American Bar Association
Standing Committee on Dispute Resolution
1800 M Street, NW
Washington, DC 20036
(202) 331-2258

National Institute for Dispute Resolution
1726 M Street, NW, Suite 500
Washington, DC 20036
(202) 466-4764

Neighbor Law, by Cora Jordan (Nolo Press). Explains the laws controlling common disputes among neighbors, involving noise, trees, property lines and fences and how to resolve disputes without a nasty lawsuit.

Safe Homes, Safe Neighborhoods, by Stephanie Mann with M.C. Blakeman (Nolo Press). Shows how neighbors can join together to stop crime and improve their neighborhoods. For example, it explains how to set up a Child Safety Committee that can resolve neighborhood disputes that pit parent against parent.

> *I was never ruined but twice—once when I lost a lawsuit, and once when I gained one.*
>
> —VOLTAIRE

Require Lawyer Impact Statements

JAPAN PRODUCES ENGINEERS TO "MAKE THE PIE BIGGER," OBSERVED FORMER HARVARD UNIVERSITY PRESIDENT DEREK BOK, WHILE AMERICA PRODUCES LAWYERS TO DIVIDE THE PIE INTO SMALLER PIECES. THE MORE LAWYERS OUR SOCIETY SUPPORTS, THE MORE LITIGIOUS WE BECOME. YET COURTS AND LEGISLATURES UNTHINKINGLY AND UNCEASINGLY PRODUCE LAWS THAT ENCOURAGE LAWYERS TO FLOURISH.

Lawyers, through their domination of courts and legislatures, seem infinitely able to mandate measures that require the services of still more lawyers. It is not uncommon to hear lawyers say, only half tongue-in-cheek, that a particular court decision or statute is a "lawyers' full employment act." They mean that many issues are left to fight about in court—or that such complicated procedures have been set up that people will be forced to hire lawyers to help them through the maze.

This problem threatens to get worse as societal change creates whole new branches of the law, each producing work for many thousands of lawyers. There are a number of well-publicized examples.

☞ Employment law: issues involving the rights of the disabled, sexual harassment, and repetitive motion injuries.

> *If the laws could speak for themselves, they would complain of lawyers.*
>
> —GEORGE SAVILE,
> ENGLISH STATESMAN

☞ Health law: issues raised by terminating life support, surrogate pregnancy and gene testing.

☞ High-tech law: issues relating to computer software patents and genetic engineering protocols.

Long-existing legal areas have also been expanded, as courts have increased the number of theories that make a person legally liable for someone else's injury. For instance, in the early days of our country, a burglar couldn't sue a landowner for injuries suffered from a fall through a rotten roof while breaking in to steal. Under current theories of liability, however, the burglar might bring—and maybe even win—such a lawsuit.

Like the courts, legislatures also guarantee lots of litigation by creating new rights and remedies that depend on courts for their enforcement. For instance, Congress recently passed a law guaranteeing family leave under a variety of circumstances, and is on the threshhold of requiring virtually all businesses to provide health-care benefits. These laws appropriately address some important issues, but enforcing them will create a lot of new work for lawyers.

Legislatures also create new work for lawyers by passing along irreconcilable differences between legislators and special interest groups to the courts. They pass the buck by writing ambiguous statutes. For example, suppose legislators can't agree on whether a new law should benefit all people who are living together as a family or only those who are married or related by blood. The warring factions may solve this impasse by using the word family—but not defining it. Hammering out the definition is left to the courts and the lawyers. Obviously, the more ambiguities legislation contains, the more lawyers are needed to resolve them.

What to Do

A good start in getting control of the lawyer glut would be to require legislatures and appeals court judges to issue a public Lawyer Impact Statement for each case or proposed new law.

This is the same general approach that is used to identify adverse environmental effects that might result from proposed development project. For most of our history, land developers could go forward with no thought to environmental consequences of their actions. Then Congress passed the National Environmental Protection Act in 1969. This law requires developers to assess and disclose, in an Environmental Impact Statement, how their proposed developments will affect the environment and why feasible alternatives that would have a less negative impact were not adopted.

Similarly, the Lawyer Impact Statement would:

☞ Reveal if a statute or court decision is likely to create more work for lawyers because it uses ambiguous terms or creates a new right or benefit that depends on lawyers to enforce.

☞ Identify possible alternatives that would require fewer lawyers—such as requiring mediation in case of a dispute, or clearly defining possible remedies.

☞ Explain why the fewer-lawyer alternatives weren't adopted.

Mandatory Lawyer Impact Statements would force legislatures and courts to publicly acknowledge when their activities are contributing to the lawyer glut. The statements would also provide groups that want to control the growth of lawyers in our society the means to target the worst lawyer-growth offenders for recall or defeat at the ballot box.

A Model Solution

Lawyer Impact Statements could be modeled after the Fiscal Impact Statements now used by several state legislatures to keep track of how big a bite each new law may take out of the state budget. Here's how they work.

Each bill to be introduced in the legislature is assessed for its possible fiscal impact on the state. If a bill requires an appropriation, risks a substantial expenditure of state funds, or might cause a substantial decrease in state revenues, it is referred to the legislature's Fiscal Committee for further study. There, a detailed dollars-and-cents analysis is made for the legislators who will ultimately vote on the bill.

The Fiscal Committee also studies the bill's potential impact on city and county budgets. If the bill requires local expenditures, it must either provide for them or expressly disclaim state responsibility for raising the funds.

Fiscal consequences identified don't by themselves kill a law, but there is at least some public accountability—and interested citizens and activists are given the information they need to assess projects intelligently.

Create a National Idea Registry

MANY OF US PRODUCE AT LEAST ONE ORIGINAL IDEA IN OUR LIFETIMES—AN IDEA THAT COULD VASTLY IMPROVE THE QUALITY OF MANY PEOPLE'S LIVES. BUT THE LAWS CONTROLLING TRADE SECRETS, PATENTS AND COPYRIGHTS ARE USUALLY INSUFFICIENT TO ENCOURAGE DEVELOPMENT OF THESE IDEAS. THE LEGAL SYSTEM TREATS MOST IDEAS, EVEN GREAT ONES, AS IF THEY HAVE NO VALUE.

Ideas are mysterious things. A wonderful plot for a novel, a brilliant product name, or a new way to open a can of peas can pop into our heads fully formed. Nothing is quite as exciting as the belief that we have produced something genuinely original.

Once the initial excitement wanes a little, our thoughts may turn to sharing the ideas with others—and possibly to fortune or at least public recognition of our brilliance.

Academic and scientific circles maintain elaborate systems for publishing original ideas and crediting their creators. Rewards come in the form of enhanced academic status and acceptance into the world of prestigious conferences and the potentially lucrative lecture circuit.

But this system rewards originality for a select few; most of us are cut out of the action. The only other outlet for good ideas is the marketplace. This is where our poor system of legal protection for ideas hurts us; it doesn't cultivate our collective creative genius.

Patent application procedures can be so complex that many people need legal assistance, which typically costs between $5,000 and $10,000. Tens of thousands more in legal costs will likely be required to enforce the patent if someone infringes it.

Trade secrets usually benefit only their large business owners, who use the economies of scale to exploit confidential information commercially. The individuals who come up with the ideas are seldom given credit, and have usually signed agreements giving the employer commercial rights over their efforts.

Copyright is sometimes thought to protect ideas. But it doesn't. Copyrights provide legal protection for the way ideas are expressed, not the ideas themselves. Of course, the first person to publish original ideas often benefits in the marketplace, but most good ideas very soon are taken over by hoards of less creative authors, composers and artists who come after.

The result is that of the millions of original ideas that flash into the world every day, only a relative few are developed into inventions or published in works protected by copyright. The rest are kept secret or lost to the public because the originator has no incentive to develop or disseminate them. And of those ideas that do see the light of day, many do not carry the name of their originators.

What to Do

As a society, we need to preserve and develop every good idea people come up with. To accomplish this, we should treat ideas as a national resource and create a National Idea Registry to record and encourage them. It could be operated by a public

> *Ideas won't keep.*
>
> —A. N. WHITEHEAD,
> ENGLISH PHILOSOPHER

nonprofit corporation. Anyone could submit any idea along with a reasonable registration fee. Each idea would be date-stamped and assigned to an examiner who was an information and research specialist.

Recognizing that some ideas are simply too bizarre to be understood by anyone other than their creator, the examiner would first screen the idea for comprehensability. If the idea passed this test, the examiner would determine whether it had been publicly expressed in modern times—as just an idea, as an invention or in an artistic or literary expression.

If an idea were determined to be original, the creator would receive an Original Idea Certificate, and the idea would be entered in a computerized database and be made available to the public at nominal cost. An inventor, author or business could use registered ideas without charge.

The Registry would reward the creator in several ways. First, the creator could use the fact of registration as a convenient way to claim authorship if the idea turned out to be important. Second, to help good ideas become known, the Registry could publish a quarterly journal featuring the best ideas received. The Registry could also award prizes to the creators of particularly promising ideas.

Like nonprofit foundations that award grants and scholarships, the Registry would have broad discretion to decide what qualified as an original idea and which ideas were rewarded or recognized. Its decisions would be final.

If the Registry listed as original some ideas that weren't, anyone could submit a 100-word statement pointing out the mistake. If convinced of its error, the Registry would enter the statement in the database.

The Idea Registry would not replace the patent, copyright and trade secret approaches. An idea examiner who felt that an idea had potential for development as an invention or use as a trade secret would give the creator an opportunity to withdraw and develop it under one of these more traditional forms of idea protection.

Computer Bulletin Boards

Electronic bulletin boards and newsgroups on the Internet and commercial online services provide excellent forums for sharing ideas. All you need is a computer and modem; most bulletin boards and newsgroups are free or charge only a nominal fee. To participate in these discussions, you call the bulletin board or newsgroup site through a modem. Once you select an appropriate topic from a menu, you can scan the contributions made by others, and if you want to jump in, you can type a comment or transmit one you've already prepared. Your contribution will appear for all to read. You can also have electronic dialogues—for days, weeks and even months—with other contributors.

Computer newsletters, magazines and bookstores all have information and materials about using what has become known as the information highway.

Encourage Mediation and Other Alternatives to Court

OUR TRIAL COURT SYSTEM JUST PLAIN DOESN'T WORK. IT'S TIME TO REPLACE IT, FOR MOST DISPUTES, WITH EFFICIENT, SENSIBLE, NON-ADVERSARIAL PROGRAM OF MEDIATION.

There are two fundamental reasons for the failure of our trial courts. First, court rules and procedures are so complicated and inefficient that lawyer fees and other costs end up being a bigger problem than the dispute itself. Second, our winner-take-all system defies logic, encourages lying and generally brings out the worst in all participants. If you hang around a law firm that specializes in litigation, you'll quickly see that the courtroom is viewed as a battlefield, where victory has little to do with fairness or even legal principles, but goes to the side that best combines trickery with aggressiveness.

Child custody disputes offer a microcosm of how a court fight leads people to spend substantial amounts of money to make things worse. Separated parents need a calm atmosphere and skilled assistance to help them agree on a cooperative way to raise their children. Recognizing this, some states now require or encourage mediation in custody or visitation disputes. (See Proposal #6, Mediate Child Custody and Support Disputes.) Parents unlucky enough to land in a court that doesn't offer mediation are faced with unfamiliar and scary courtrooms, expensive lawyers trained and often itching to fight and judges who usually have no training in resolving domestic disputes. Too often, this trial-by-battle-like procedure encourages both parents to see and attempt to portray a complicated family relationship, full of shades of gray, in dichotomous terms: winning full custody is good and losing it is evil.

Normally, this take-no-prisoners approach encourages each side to escalate the battle, which in turn typically leads to more court procedures and bigger lawyer bills. Only when the parents have no more money to pay their lawyers does the battle end. By this time, the hateful things said by both sides in the heat of the court battle forever stand in the way of adopting a decent parenting plan.

The lottery-like nature of trial is another serious failing. Ask any business person about the prospect of a contested case—even one in which he or she is convinced he or she is right—and you're almost sure to get an earful. The business person not only resents the fearful burden of cost and time involved, but is even more terrified by the utter unpredictability of the outcome. A big loss may even threaten the financial viability of the business. It's an expensive paranoia, because it often causes businesses to buy their way out of even the most meritless claims.

By contrast, mediation, where the parties must themselves agree to the resolution of their dispute, bypasses most of the delays, endless procedures and attorney fees associated with any contested court case. But that's not its biggest advantage. Because no result can be imposed on the parties, mediation largely eliminates the fear and loss of control that pervade our trial court system.

Whenever mediation has been tried—whether for neighbor disputes, divorce, child custody or business disputes—it's worked. Disputants, with the help of a mediator, have a chance to calmly fashion a joint solution they can live with. In fact, mediation has become so successful that thousands of people

> *Those lawyers with Hah-*
> *vud accents are always*
> *thinking up new ways to*
> *take advantage of people.*
>
> —HARRY TRUMAN

(some of them lawyers) now advocate its widespread application as an alternative to contested court cases.

If mediation is so great, it's fair to ask why it hasn't already replaced court battles. In a nutshell, the answer is that organized trial lawyers and others who reap huge profits from fighting in court vitriolically oppose it. This is hardly surprising, since in mediation, lawyers are either bypassed entirely or take on a far more limited role as advisors to the peacemaking process. In short, their ability to collect large fees is greatly reduced.

What to Do

Every trial court in America should make available reasonably priced, accessible and comprehensive mediation alternatives for all types of contested cases. In areas such as child custody and visitation, mediation should be required, as is already the case in some states. Only if the parents can't work out a settlement with the help of a mediator should the dispute end up in a courtroom.

Mediators can be either or both court employees and private contractors. They should have training and experience both in mediation techniques and, if the dispute involves technically complicated issues, in the substantive area of the dispute.

For big-dollar cases, other alternatives to contested court fights should also be available. For example, a procedure called "early neutral evaluation," which invites a neutral expert to evaluate the merits of a complicated lawsuit, can be of great assistance, to allow the parties to negotiate or mediate a solution.

All available mediation programs should be widely promoted, as is now done in a few courts. For example, the fact that mediation is available should be clearly communicated in writing to all parties to every lawsuit filed in the court, along with material emphasizing how mediation can save money and time and let the parties arrive at a mutually agreed-upon settlement. And before any client agrees to a lawsuit, the lawyer should give him or her a written estimate of the fees it's likely to generate.

Mediation in Maine: Small Claims Court

In Maine, every contested small claims court case is referred to a public mediation program. Mediators—people from all walks of life (including the legal profession) who have taken a state-sponsored training course—are available right in the courthouse. The mediator's role is to help the parties work out a mutually-agreeable settlement. More than half the time this works, and no court fight is necessary. When mediation fails and the parties cannot arrive at their own settlement, cases are referred back to small claims court and decided by a judge.

Because mediators are paid less than judges and do not need the same level of support staff, mediation is proving to be cost-effective.

Apply the First Amendment to Legal Information

LAWYERS LIKE TO KEEP LEGAL INFORMATION CLOSE TO THEIR VESTS AND GIVE IT OUT ONLY FOR A FEE. THAT'S THEIR RIGHT AS BUSINESS PEOPLE. BUT TO USE THE COURTS TO KEEP OTHERS FROM DISSEMINATING THIS INFORMATION IS NOT ONLY NASTY—IT'S A CLEAR VIOLATION OF THE FIRST AMENDMENT.

Information—especially information about how to approach and use the organs of our government—is the lifeblood of a democracy. The more freely such information flows, the better the democracy works. Blockages tend to unfairly concentrate power in the hands of the privileged.

Today we face a legal access crisis because information about how to approach and use our courts moves sluggishly if at all. It is dammed up by a class of professionals known as lawyers. In all states except Arizona, lawyers have used their power to enact statutes restricting to lawyers the right to provide legal information designed to solve an individual's legal needs. And in all but a few states, the laws go on to provide that a non-lawyer who gives legal advice has committed a crime punishable by imprisonment.

Almost no other type of speech has ever been forbidden in advance to the public in this way. The reason is clear. Prohibitions on speech are almost always ruled to be unconstitional violations of the First Amendment, which forbids any law that abridges the freedom of speech. This is especially true when it comes to speech about how to deal with public bodies such as Congress, state legislatures and administrative agencies. There is no good reason to treat the courts differently than other parts of government are treated.

Courts have allowed only a handful of narrow exceptions to this near-absolute rule prohibiting advance restrictions to free speech. Obscenity, incitement to violence and false speech (libel, slander, fraud) are examples of the kinds of speech that the government may legally abridge. The government also may restrict commercial speech, such as advertising, if the restriction directly serves substantial state interests and the restriction is in reasonable proportion to the interests served.

If speech does not fall within these types of exceptions, it is fully protected under the First Amendment. It may be restricted only if the government has a compelling interest for doing so and the restriction is as narrowly tailored as possible to satisfy the compelling interest.

The U.S. Supreme Court has ruled that legal advice is fully protected speech, rather than commercial speech, even though the legal advice is given for a fee. (*Board of Trustees, State University of New York v. Fox*, 492 U.S. 469 (1989).) That means that the government must have a compelling interest in stopping non-lawyers from giving legal advice. It's a tough standard to meet.

Consumer protection is the reason usually advanced by the legal profession to justify handing it the exclusive right to give legal advice. According to this view, poor legal advice can cause such

What do bakers and lawyers have in common?

They both like to carve up the pie.

> *At the rate law schools are turning them out, by the year 2000 there will be more lawyers than humans.*

serious harm that a license should be required of those who provide it. Numerous studies of this issue, however, have shown that this fear is unwarranted. No study has produced concrete evidence that legal advice from non-lawyers causes more harm than that sold by licensed lawyers.

Denying consumers who can't afford a lawyer the right to buy legal advice from more affordable sources is a ridiculous way to protect them. The argument put forth by lawyers' groups seems to be that it is better for most consumers to have no legal advice than for some to receive advice that may be wrong. Interestingly, this argument is raised by lawyers, almost never by consumers. Lawyers persist in making it even though there have been very few complaints about existing non-lawyer legal form preparation businesses. It's as if accountants and tax lawyers could put H&R Block and other tax preparers out of business because they didn't approve of their training or advice.

Thus there seems to be no compelling reason to deny non-lawyers the right to offer the public information about our laws and courts. But even if there were a compelling interest, the method of regulation—barring everyone but lawyers from giving legal advice—is much broader than it needs to be. For example, the term "legal advice" is never clearly defined in the laws that forbid non-lawyers from giving it. This means that when a complaint against a non-lawyer is made, a judge (also a lawyer, of course) has no standard to go by when deciding whether or not legal advice was given. As a result, these laws make criminals out of anyone who utters words that might, even after the fact, be interpreted as legal advice by a court. This sort of blanket censorship of all unlicensed legal advice is as blatant a violation of the First Amendment as you'll ever find.

What to Do

States should continue to regulate the legal profession even as they decriminalize legal advice by non-lawyers. People who wish to call themselves lawyers and represent others in court would still have to qualify for this privilege. However, people who choose not to go this route would not be prosecuted for giving legal advice.

This is a workable, sensible system; it is exactly the way most states now regulate the accounting profession. You may call yourself a Certified Public Accountant if you meet the state's qualifications; otherwise you are free to give tax preparation, bookkeeping or accounting advice as long as you don't use the CPA label. Consumers are free to choose a CPA, and pay a higher rate for the expertise the label carries with it, or consult someone without the CPA credential, who probably charges less.

But what happens if a non-lawyer provides poor service or gives bad advice? If a customer loses money because of wrong legal advice given by a non-lawyer, the complaint could and should be addressed under the same consumer protection rules that are applied to other similar businesses. Dissatisfied customers could sue in small claims or regular court for damages, or ask local prosecutors—or a specialized regulatory agency if one exists—to shut down businesses that make a practice of dispensing shoddy legal advice.

> *Lawyers: Persons who write a 10,000 word document and call it a brief.*
>
> —FRANZ KAFKA

Appoint Non-Lawyers as Judges

THE IDEA THAT JUDGES SHOULD BE LAWYERS IS DEEPLY INGRAINED IN AMERICAN CULTURE—SO MUCH SO THAT IN SOME STATES, LAWS DON'T ALLOW ANYONE ELSE TO BE CONSIDERED. BUT PICKING ALL OF OUR JUDGES FROM ONE PROFESSIONAL GROUP RESULTS IN A SYSTEM THAT COSTS TOO MUCH, IS BIASED AGAINST NON-LAWYER PARTICIPATION AND OFTEN PRODUCES POOR QUALITY JUDGING.

As a group, lawyers do not have the knowledge and skills needed to handle many of the issues routinely presented to them in our courts. To understand why, spend a few days at a law school. You'll find that future judges are taught to solve all legal problems by using a formalistic system of analysis and a database consisting of a mish-mash of old court cases. Unlike other professions and occupations whose educational methods have changed radically at least once a decade to reflect new knowledge, law school education has changed remarkably little since World War I.

Traditionalists claim that this is as it should be, since immutable legal principles derived from basic truths about human behavior need no revision. But critics more cogently point out that the best way to predict which side will win a particular case is to know the politics and prejudices of the judge, not the intricacies of the law.

One quaint notion almost universally embraced by our judiciary is that good decisions can be arrived at by applying traditional legal doctrines without the need to understand the technical issues that underlie the dispute. For example, judges feel absolutely comfortable deciding a case involving the alleged theft of a new process to increase the output of a power plant, even if they don't have a clue about how a steam turbine works. Perhaps a better example is lawsuits over software patents—an area in which judges who can't use a word processor, let alone explain how a computer works, confidently make highly technical decisions with financial implications that run to billions of dollars.

By the time a lawyer is appointed to the bench, she has probably been out of law school at least 20 years. During those years, chances are she has specialized in one or a few narrow areas of practice. A corporate lawyer appointed to criminal court, a tax lawyer put in charge of child custody decisions—it happens all the time. Judges who have been given their jobs as a reward for political loyalty are woefully unprepared to handle a broad array of legal problems.

But surely lawyers receive additional training when they become judges? Don't count on it. Except for a few brief cram courses after they are appointed to the bench, new judges are largely on their own. Put more bluntly, if your average veterinarian were as poorly trained as your average judge, you wouldn't let Bowser within 100 feet of him.

Against this background, it hardly seems a radical notion that many non-lawyers, given the right training, might make better

Lawyer: A mouth with a life-support system.

> *What's the difference between a catfish and a lawyer?*
>
> *One is a bottom-dwelling, garbage-eating scavenger. The other is a fish.*

judges than do our current crop of lawyers. Disputes involving technical subjects such as medical malpractice or multimedia copyrights, areas in which most lawyers are hopelessly ignorant, offer obvious examples of legal areas where a non-lawyer with an understanding of the underlying technology might well make a better decision.

Consider another of our courts' most common concerns: family law. In every county in America, on every business day, judges make immensely important decisions involving the custody, visitation and support of children. But because most family court judges haven't practiced in this area, they have absolutely no practical experience with either the legal or interpersonal issues involved.

They didn't learn it in law school, either. Surprisingly, in most American law schools, zero time is spent on the personal and family dynamics of divorce; the one or, at most, two family law courses most law students take focus almost exclusively on who gets the money and property. Even that information is badly out-of-date long before a law school grad is appointed to the bench.

What about on-the-job training? A few new family court judges learn quickly and so aren't incompetent long. Many don't. Precisely because family court is a high-stress, emotion-filled environment that they are not prepared to handle, most judges try to move on to other types of cases as soon as possible—often after only one year. In short, few judges are around long enough to climb the learning curve to real competence, and there is no continuity in an area that cries out for it.

Divorce lawyers understand that fast turnover, coupled with little or no training, offers a unique opportunity to shop for a more agreeable judge. They often bring the same custody and visitation cases back into court again and again. Sooner or later, an inexperienced new judge with no personal knowledge of what happened before may make a different decision.

The need for more a competent, responsive judiciary isn't the only reason to open the job to non-lawyers. There is a second fundamental reason to break the legal profession's stranglehold over our courts. Given our system of government, in which the judicial branch has constitutional power to control our entire legal and justice system, allowing the legal profession to monopolize the judiciary all but guarantees the continuation of the law profession's self-interested tyranny over our entire legal system.

The unhappy result is on daily display in America's courthouses. Precisely because judges are all lawyers and believe that non-lawyers have no place in our courts, there are few forms, instructions or pamphlets available to help citizens accomplish even the simplest legal tasks. If confused non-lawyers ask for any information beyond the location of the bathroom, judges far too often just shrug and tell them to see an attorney. (See Proposal #41, Stop Discrimination Against Non-Lawyers in the Courts.)

Having only lawyers as judges also severely hampers citizens' rights to purchase basic affordable legal services from trained non-lawyers, often called legal technicians or independent paralegals. More and more consumers know about this affordable alternative to lawyers and want to patronize reasonably-priced paralegal services. But lawyers—instead of meeting the competition by lowering fees and improving service—appeal to their black-robed brethren to stamp out non-lawyer competitors. Many judges respond in one of two ways. Some attempt to enforce laws, passed by lawyer-dominated legislatures in the

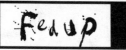

1930s, that make it illegal to practice law without a license. Others attempt to do the same thing, by resurrecting a centuries-old legal doctrine known as "inherent judicial powers," to claim that judges have the constitutional power to not only regulate the courts, but all law-related transactions. (See Proposal #28, End the Lawyer Monopoly: Bring Competition to the Law Business.)

In the scurry to prevent non-lawyers from competing with lawyers, judges rarely bother to examine the quality of their work. So, for example, even if a non-lawyer does a better job typing divorce papers for $100 than a lawyer does for $1,000, the non-lawyer is likely to go to jail while the lawyer goes to lunch with the judge.

Prejudice in favor of lawyers by a lawyer-controlled judiciary also takes other destructive forms. One is overcharging. In many types of cases, judges control or influence how much lawyers will be paid. Because of close personal and professional relationships—and because many judges well remember when they were hustling for fees—these awards are often far too high.

What to Do

A great democratic wind would blow across our justice system if we would simply do away with the requirement that judges be lawyers. A better approach would be to establish standards of relevant education and work experience and open up the occupation to anyone who qualifies. If tests are given, they should be based on the kind of disputes that will come before the judges and not be a rehash of what passes for legal education.

For family court judges, qualifications might include training in the social sciences, with concentration on coursework on how post-divorce families can best work to raise healthy children. Mediation skills—taught in depth in only a few law schools—and coursework in the economic aspects of divorce should also be required.

Supplement this background with a six-month intensive course on domestic relations law before allowing judges to pick up the gavel, and there is no doubt that they would have a better grasp of these cases than do today's poorly-trained lawyer-judges. And because these non-lawyer judges would be expected to make their careers in the family courts, they would have a chance to improve their skills and knowledge with time.

Finally, because this new breed of non-lawyer judges would not be part of the local lawyer-buddy network, they would be much more likely to award lower fees. As a result, courts would be more affordable as well as fair.

One lawsuit begets another.

—Latin proverb

Stop Discrimination Against Non-Lawyers in the Courts

THE AMERICAN LEGAL SYSTEM REMAINS A STRONGHOLD OF RESISTANCE TO THE DEFINING IDEAL THAT ALL AMERICANS ARE ENTITLED TO EQUAL TREATMENT. PEOPLE WHO APPEAR IN COURT ON THEIR OWN BEHALF (CALLED "PRO PER" OR "PRO SE") ARE LIKELY TO BE TREATED AS THIRD-CLASS CITIZENS BY LAWYERS AND JUDGES.

Discrimination against people because they are members of an unpopular group is always nasty—especially when it denies them fundamental rights, such as a job, a decent education or a freely-chosen place to live. The United States' powerful commitment to fight discrimination based on race, sex and age, to mention just a few, defines what is best about our nation in the second half of the 20th century.

But discriminatory treatment against anyone who attempts to represent herself in court goes way beyond unfriendliness. (See Proposal #5, Make the Courthouse User-Friendly.) Indeed, hostile judges regularly rule against pro pers unfairly or misapply nit-picking procedural rules, freezing pro pers out of the legal system.

Nastiness directed at pro pers often begins in the court clerk's office, where employees—reflecting the hostile attitudes of their judicial superiors—typically give non-lawyers substandard service. For example, court clerks who will graciously provide a confused lawyer with step-by-step guidance about an arcane procedural rule will turn right around and reject a far more basic question of a pro per. All the non-lawyer gets is a peremptory nod at a prominent sign reading Court Clerks Cannot Give Legal Advice—For a Referral to a Lawyer, Call the County Bar Association.

This mean-spirited attitude toward the public often gets worse in the courtroom. Lawyers, even those who come running in ten minutes late, usually have their cases heard first. And when the pro per finally does get a turn, the judge is all too likely to have a patronizing attitude and a closed mind. Someone who asks that an impenetrable hunk of legal jargon be translated into English or makes a small, easily-corrected mistake, or even hesitates a second too long is likely to be tongue-lashed for clogging the court's busy schedule and told, in no uncertain terms, to get a lawyer.

Judges often defend the way they treat non-lawyers by comparing themselves to a baseball umpire suddenly faced with novice players who don't know the rules. "We do the best we can under difficult circumstances," they claim.

Nonsense. Most organized sports welcome novices and go to great lengths to explain the rules to them. After all, it's counterproductive to keep potential customers ignorant and at arm's length. If courts did half as well in fulfilling their more fundamental duty to provide all citizens with reasonable legal access, tens of millions of Americans would be comfortable representing themselves.

Unfortunately, as long as we let former lawyers—people who have been trained to profit from the present opaque system—

control every aspect of our courts, citizen access is unlikely to improve. Just try to remember the last time you saw a judge run a clinic for pro pers or establish a separate day to hear non-lawyer cases. Unless you live in one of very few places in America where individual judges dare to bypass the lawyer cartel and attempt to open the courthouse to all, the answer is never. In fact, just the idea that a judge should have the responsibility to welcome and assist those who can't afford a lawyer is shocking to most judges and lawyers.

To take just a few examples of how our present judicial system discriminates against non-lawyers, consider that:

☞ The great majority of issues considered by a judge, such as adoptions and probates, are unopposed. Usually success is assured by the right paperwork. Yet no effort is made to provide easy-to-understand forms and instructions.

☞ To master substantive law and legal procedure, people need access to good information. Yet little work—apart from the individual efforts of a few dedicated law librarians—is done to make law libraries and their materials accessible and understandable to the public. (See Proposal #21, Help Non-Lawyers Use Law Libraries.)

☞ Even though a significant number of judges and clerks are routinely and insultingly hostile to pro pers, absolutely nothing is done to change their behavior or discipline them.

To give Americans a decent chance to cope with their routine legal problems without a lawyer, a radical change in judicial attitude is needed—and needed fast. But no relief seems near. Although our supposedly learned lawyers are quick to

> *If you want to find the law, go to law school. If you want to find justice, go to small claims court.*
>
> — PAUL ROSENTHAL, FORMER LEGAL AID LAWYER

appoint commissions to look into claims of discrimination by minority or female attorneys, for the most part they don't even understand how badly they treat the general public.

It's way past time they found out.

What to Do

Start by recognizing that better treatment of pro pers won't come quickly or easily, since most judges and clerks don't even recognize the problem. Similarly, appointing a significant number of non-lawyers to the bench—surely the best way to root out discrimination against prop pers—is unlikely to happen anytime soon. (See Proposal #40, Appoint Non-Lawyers as Judges.)

In the meantime, we are left with small steps. Probably the most effective would be for each court to appoint advisory groups made up of pro pers, just as they currently work formally and informally with lawyer groups. These pro per advisors should be given a clear mandate to suggest ways to make non-lawyers welcome and effective in our courts. (See Proposal5, Make the Courthouse User-Friendly.) And when they do, even if their suggestions involve major changes in the way court business is conducted, they should be listened to.

It Shouldn't Hurt to Be a Pro Per

What strikes you first about Judge Roderic Duncan's room is that it's a homey place—for a courtroom. Wedged between the customary flags and pictures of eagles is a poster bearing the slogan "It Shouldn't Hurt To Be a Family."

Most of those scheduled for Wednesday morning hearings in the Alameda County, California courtroom appear as pro pers, representing themselves instead of hiring an attorney. Most seek court orders for child support, visitation or custody.

If there is a contested custody arrangement, the couple usually meets first with a representative from the Family Support Division to work out a compromise that is in the best interest of the child or children. Then, using a benchtop computer, Judge Duncan computes child support payments on the spot. He patiently explains how the payments will increase or decrease if custody arrangements change.

In Duncan's courtroom, lawyers often seem superfluous. Sometimes advice gets offered by family members and friends who come along and offer support to those who appear. "Stand up and go show him your pay stub," a woman stagewhispers from the back of the courtroom to a man seeking lower child support payments. She is quickly silenced by an admonishing shush from the court sheriff.

Here, on Wednesday mornings the essential paperwork is prepared for pro pers by a volunteer law student, who writes out the judgment reached in each case, gets it signed by the judge and hands it to each pro per. On a typical Wednesday morning, the student fills out the orders in about 25 family law cases. Many would never realize that obtaining that piece of paper is necessary to make a court judgment legal. Of course, they could hire a lawyer to do it—at the going rate of $150.

Free Lawyers to Help Self-Helpers: 'Unbundle' Legal Services

AT LEAST 150 MILLION AMERICANS CAN'T AFFORD TO HIRE LAWYERS TO MEET ALL THEIR LEGAL NEEDS. WE NEED TO ENABLE LAWYERS TO HELP THESE PEOPLE HELP THEMSELVES.

That most people can't afford lawyers should come as no surprise; just compare the $150 to $250 hourly fee commonly charged by lawyers with the hourly wage of the average person.

In response to this crisis, large numbers of Americans are attempting to handle their own legal work, especially routine tasks such as divorce, bankruptcy, wills and probate. To guide them, many use self-help law books and software, or hire independent paralegals—non-lawyers who offer help with legal paperwork for a fraction of what lawyers charge. An American Bar Association study showed that in Maricopa County, Arizona (Phoenix), in 1990, 92% of divorces were handled with either no lawyer or only one lawyer.

The growth of high-quality self-help resources and paralegal services is to the good, but they don't entirely meet the public's need for affordable legal help. Sometimes, people need a lawyer's expertise or a bit of personalized advice when a glitch threatens to develop. Sadly, it's usually hard to come by. Lawyers rarely

> *When there are too many lawyers, there can be no justice.*
>
> —LIN YUTANG

agree to coach self-helpers or step in to provide limited help when needed; usually, they either insist on either taking over the entire case or staying out completely.

Lawyers tend to resist helping people cope with their own legal problems for a couple of reasons. First, they tend to distrust the very idea of self-help law. Second, they are scared of being sued over aspects of the case they have no control over.

This fear is understandable. Bar association rules and decisions by courts reinforce this all-or-nothing approach, and lawyers naturally feel intimidated. There are unfortunate consequences for both lawyers and for self-helpers. Consider the following example:

In the course of handling their own divorce, Joe and Eileen Alvarez find that they need some help from an attorney on splitting up their house, pension plans and other valuable property. They approach lawyer Warren Willis and ask him to help them draw up a property division agreement. Willis declines to help them, explaining that his ethical and professional responsibilities prevent him from handling cases piecemeal. The Alvarezes must either hire him to handle the entire divorce or go it alone. Because they can't afford full representation but also are uncomfortable about proceeding without help, the Alvarezes are in a tight spot. But they aren't the only losers. Lawyer Willis, who has just turned down paying clients, not only suffers a loss of revenue, but also the opportunity to build his business by getting future referrals from satisfied customers.

What to Do

Lawyers must recognize that self-help law is here to stay. And to meet the needs of clients who wish to help themselves, lawyers must "unbundle" their services and offer potential clients a variety of options, so people can buy only what they need.

For example, one client might need information, but not representation. Another may want the attorney to review documents, not draft them. And as more and more disputes go to simplified arbitration instead of trial, many people wish to handle the hearing themselves. But they nevertheless may want to pay a lawyer for an hour or two of general advice and help with preparation before the hearing.

Despite legal strictures that prohibit or at least discourage it, a few lawyers have already set up businesses that offer customers a range of unbundled legal services. Here are some examples:

☞ *Divorce Help Line.* A telephone/fax service in Santa Cruz, California, Divorce Help Line has a standard price list for divorce-related legal advice over the phone, as well as for document preparation and the review of documents prepared by self-helpers. Computerized child support calculations and telephone mediation services are among an extensive list of services available.

☞ *TeleLawyer.* This telephone service offers legal information and advice, telephone seminars on a broad range of legal subjects, referrals to self-help law materials and referrals to lawyers who have agreed to provide certain services at a low flat rate.

☞ *The Law Store.* This storefront in Palo Alto, California sells self-help legal publications and makes paralegal and lawyer services available to customers who want additional advice, document preparation or other legal services.

These efforts to unbundle traditional legal services are just a start. With a little imagination they could be taken much further. For instance, instead of just offering to represent spouses in a divorce, a lawyer might offer a menu of services that would look something like this:

Service	Fee
Self-help law book covering the basics of state divorce law and court forms	$24.95
Paralegal assistance in filling in and filing court forms	$10 per form or $40 per hour
Legal information and counsel about divorce and court procedure	$80 per hour
Lawyer review of all forms prepared by client	$150
Telephone consultations with lawyer	$2 per minute
Mediation of child custody and visitation issues	$200 per session of four hours or less
Representation in a deposition or court proceeding, including preparation time and appearance	$150 per hour
Lawyer review of mediation agreement that settles major issues of the divorce	$150
Full representation of one party in an uncontested divorce	$750
Full representation of one party in a contested divorce	$1,500 plus $100 per hour for all time over 10 hours

A similar approach could be taken by lawyers who specialize in bankruptcy, litigation, estate planning, small business law or intellectual property. Just as with divorce, each of these areas could be broken down into a menu of discrete services.

Another way of conceptualizing how lawyers can work with clients is to see the lawyer in the role of a coach. Instead of handling a whole legal task, the coach helps the client find and master legal information and is available to provide advice and other services. For example, the owner of a small business, who can't afford to pay a lawyer to prepare an employee handbook, might use self-help resources suggested by the lawyer to come up with a first draft. The lawyer could then review it and suggest improvements at a reasonable cost.

Before lawyers can offer unbundled services and act as self-help law coaches, they will need some coaching themselves. Law school courses on the role of the lawyer should be augmented to include these approaches.

Some major institutional barriers to unbundling legal services this way will also need to fall. One such barrier is lawyers' general presumption that a lawyer should control a case because of the lawyer's superior knowledge and experience. But the more lawyers are willing to encourage their clients to handle at least some of their own legal work, the faster these clients will become legally savvy. And the more savvy consumers become, the more they will be able to accept responsibility for their cases, and the easier it will be for lawyers to let them drive the relationship.

Another barrier to unbundling legal services is that lawyers are afraid they will be held professionally or financially responsible for what they *don't* do. For instance, suppose a lawyer helps someone file a form in court, and later it turns out that a different strategy would have yielded better results. If the self-helper can sue the lawyer for not recommending the alternate strategy, most

What do lawyers use for birth control?

Their personalities.

lawyers will be unwilling to offer limited help.

To address this problem, laws governing professional liability and ethics should be amended. Lawyers should specifically be allowed to contract with a customer to provide limited services, without being legally responsible for failing to provide additional services not requested by the client.

For example, a lawyer might agree to prepare and file a motion (request to the court) for $200 or review one prepared by a self-helper for $75. Either way, the lawyer-customer agreement would specify that the lawyer would competently perform the service requested, but would not be liable for any consequences of the client's self-representation.

more books from Nolo Press

ESTATE PLANNING & PROBATE

Make Your Own Living Trust, Clifford	1st Ed	$19.95	LITR
Plan Your Estate, Clifford	3rd Ed	$24.95	NEST
Nolo's Simple Will Book, Clifford	2nd Ed	$17.95	SWIL
Who Will Handle Your Finances If You Can't?, Clifford & Randolph	1st Ed	$19.95	FINA
The Conservatorship Book (California), Goldoftas & Farren	2nd Ed	$29.95	CNSV
How to Probate an Estate (California), Nissley	7th Ed	$34.95	PAE
Nolo's Law Form Kit: Wills, Clifford & Goldoftas	1st Ed	$14.95	KWL
Write Your Will (audio cassette), Warner & Greene	1st Ed	$14.95	TWYW
5 Ways to Avoid Probate (audio cassette), Warner & Greene	1st Ed	$14.95	TPRO

PLAN
YOUR
ESTATE

by attorneys Denis Clifford & Cora Jordan

The most comprehensive guide to estate planning available from basic techniques to sophisticated tax savings strategies

NOLO PRESS SELF-HELP LAW

GOING TO COURT

Represent Yourself in Court, Bergman & Berman-Barrett	1st Ed	$29.95	RYC
Everybody's Guide to Municipal Court (California), Duncan	1st Ed	$29.95	MUNI
Everybody's Guide to Small Claims Court (California), Warner	11th Ed	$18.95	CSCC
Everybody's Guide to Small Claims Court (National), Warner	5th Ed	$18.95	NSCC
Fight Your Ticket (California), Brown	5th Ed	$18.95	FYT
Collect Your Court Judgment (California), Scott, Elias & Goldoftas	2nd Ed	$19.95	JUDG
How to Change Your Name (California), Loeb & Brown	6th Ed	$24.95	NAME
The Criminal Records Book (California), Siegel	3rd Ed	$19.95	CRIM
Winning in Small Claims Court, Warner & Greene (audio cassette)	1st Ed	$14.95	TWIN

more books from Nolo Press

BUSINESS & WORKPLACE

 Taking Care of Your Corporation,
   Vol. I: Director & Shareholder Meetings Made Easy, Mancuso 1st Ed $26.95   CORK

 Software Development: A Legal Guide, Fishman   1st Ed $44.95   SFT

The Legal Guide for Starting & Running a Small Business,
   Steingold   1st Ed $22.95   RUNS

Sexual Harassment on the Job, Petrocelli & Repa   1st Ed $14.95   HARS

Your Rights in the Workplace, Repa   2nd Ed $15.95   YRW

How to Write a Business Plan, McKeever   4th Ed $19.95   SBS

Marketing Without Advertising, Phillips & Rasberry   1st Ed $14.00   MWAD

The Partnership Book, Clifford & Warner   4th Ed $24.95   PART'

The California Nonprofit Corporation Handbook, Mancuso   6th Ed $29.95   NON

 The California Nonprofit Corporation Handbook, Mancuso   DOS $39.95   NPI
  MAC $39.95   NPM

 How to Form a Nonprofit Corporation (National), Mancuso   DOS $39.95   NNP

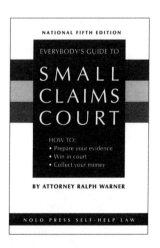

 = BOOKS WITH DISK

TO ORDER CALL 800-992-6656

CATALOG

How to Form Your Own California Corporation, Mancuso	7th Ed	$29.95	CCOR
How to Form Your Own California Corporation with Corporate Records Binder and Disk, Mancuso	1st Ed	$39.95	CACI
The California Professional Corporation Handbook, Mancuso	5th Ed	$34.95	PROF
How to Form Your Own Florida Corporation, Mancuso	DOS	$39.95	FLCO
How to Form Your Own New York Corporation, Mancuso	DOS	$39.95	NYCI
How to Form Your Own Texas Corporation, Mancuso	4th Ed	$29.95	TCOR
How to Form Your Own Texas Corporation, Mancuso	DOS	$39.95	TCI
The Independent Paralegal's Handbook, Warner	3rd Ed	$29.95	PARA
Getting Started as an Independent Paralegal, Warner (audio cassette)	2nd Ed	$44.95	GSIP
How to Start Your Own Business: Small Business Law, Warner & Greene (audio cassette)	1st Ed	$14.95	TBUS

THE NEIGHBORHOOD

Neighbor Law: Fences, Trees, Boundaries & Noise, Jordan	1st Ed	$14.95	NEI
Safe Home, Safe Neighborhoods: Stopping Crime Where You Live, Mann & Blakeman	1st Ed	$14.95	SAFE
Dog Law, Randolph	2nd Ed	$12.95	DOG

 = BOOKS WITH DISK

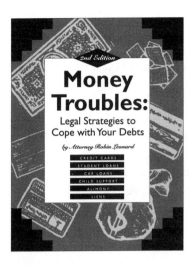

MONEY MATTERS

Stand Up to the IRS, Daily	2nd Ed	$21.95	SIRS
Money Troubles: Legal Strategies to Cope With Your Debts, Leonard	2nd Ed	$16.95	MT
How to File for Bankruptcy, Elias, Renauer & Leonard	4th Ed	$25.95	HFB
Simple Contracts for Personal Use, Elias & Stewart	2nd Ed	$16.95	CONT
Nolo's Law Form Kit: Power of Attorney, Clifford, Randolph & Goldoftas	1st Ed	$14.95	KPA
Nolo's Law Form Kit: Personal Bankruptcy, Elias, Renauer, Leonard & Goldoftas	1st Ed	$14.95	KBNK
Nolo's Law Form Kit: Rebuild Your Credit, Leonard & Goldoftas	1st Ed	$14.95	KCRD
Nolo's Law Form Kit: Loan Agreements, Stewart & Goldoftas	1st Ed	$14.95	KLOAN
Nolo's Law Form Kit: Buy & Sell Contracts, Elias, Stewart & Goldoftas	1st Ed	$9.95	KCONT

CATALOG

FAMILY MATTERS

Smart Ways to Save Money During & After Divorce, Collins & Wall	1st	$14.95	SAVMO
How to Raise or Lower Child Support In California, Duncan & Siegel	2nd Ed	$17.95	CHLD
Divorce & Money, Woodhouse & Collins with Blakeman	2nd Ed	$21.95	DIMO
The Living Together Kit, Ihara & Warner	6th Ed	$17.95	LTK
The Guardianship Book (California), Goldoftas & Brown	1st Ed	$19.95	GB
A Legal Guide for Lesbian and Gay Couples, Curry & Clifford	8th Ed	$24.95	LG
How to Do Your Own Divorce in California, Sherman	19th Ed	$21.95	CDIV
Practical Divorce Solutions, Sherman	1st Ed	$14.95	PDS
California Marriage & Divorce Law, Warner, Ihara & Elias	11th Ed	$19.95	MARR
How to Adopt Your Stepchild in California, Zagone & Randolph	4th Ed	$22.95	ADOP
Nolo's Pocket Guide to Family Law, Leonard & Elias	3rd Ed	$14.95	FLD
Divorce: A New Yorker's Guide to Doing it Yourself, Alexandra	1st Ed	$24.95	NYDIV

JUST FOR FUN

29 Reasons Not to Go to Law School, Warner & Ihara	4th Ed	$9.95	29R
Devil's Advocates, Roth & Roth	1st Ed	$12.95	DA
Poetic Justice, Roth & Roth	1st Ed	$9.95	PJ

29 Reasons Not to Go to Law School

This book can save you three years, $70,000 and your sanity.

BEFORE L.S.   AFTER L.S.

by Ralph Warner & Toni Ihara, Illustrated by Mari Stein

3RD EDITION • OVER 80,000 COPIES SOLD

PATENT IT YOURSELF

BY PATENT ATTORNEY DAVID PRESSMAN

CONTAINS ALL THE FORMS AND INSTRUCTIONS
NECESSARY TO PATENT YOUR INVENTION IN THE U.S.

NOLO PRESS SELF-HELP LAW

"PATENT IT YOURSELF is a top-notch reference for patent and trademark information."
The San Francisco Examiner

PATENT, COPYRIGHT & TRADEMARK

Trademark: How to Name Your Business & Product, McGrath & Elias, with Shena	1st Ed	$29.95	TRD
Patent It Yourself, Pressman	3rd Ed	$39.95	PAT
The Inventor's Notebook, Grissom & Pressman	1st Ed	$19.95	INOT
The Copyright Handbook, Fishman	2nd Ed	$24.95	COHA

LANDLORDS & TENANTS

The Landlord's Law Book, Vol. 1: Rights & Responsibilities (California), Brown & Warner	4th Ed	$32.95	LBRT
The Landlord's Law Book, Vol. 2: Evictions (California), Brown	4th Ed	$32.95	LBEV
Tenants' Rights (California), Moskovitz & Warner	11th Ed	$15.95	CTEN
Nolo's Law Form Kit: Leases & Rental Agreements (California), Warner & Stewart	1st Ed	$14.95	KLEAS

CATALOG

HOMEOWNERS

How to Buy a House in California, Warner, Serkes & Devine	3rd Ed	$24.95	BHCA
For Sale By Owner, Devine	2nd Ed	$24.95	FSBO
Homestead Your House, Warner, Sherman & Ihara	8th Ed	$9.95	HOME
The Deeds Book, Randolph	2nd Ed	$15.95	DEED

OLDER AMERICANS

Beat the Nursing Home Trap: A Consumer's Guide to Choosing & Financing Long Term Care, Matthews	2nd Ed	$18.95	ELD
Social Security, Medicare & Pensions, Matthews with Berman	5th Ed	$18.95	SOA

RESEARCH/REFERENCE

Legal Research: How to Find & Understand the Law, Elias & Levinkind	3rd Ed	$19.95	LRES
Legal Research Made Easy: A Roadmap Through the Law Library Maze (2½ hr videotape & manual), Nolo & Legal Star	1st Ed	$89.95	LRME

OVER 50,000 SOLD / THIRD EDITION

LEGAL RESEARCH
How To Find and Understand the Law

BY ATTORNEYS STEPHEN ELIAS & SUSAN LEVINKIND

A step-by-step method for answering legal questions

• Learn how to use the law library
• Find statues, regulations and cases
• Understand how the legal system works

NOLO PRESS SELF-HELP LAW

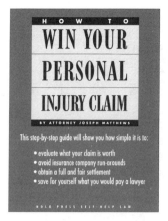

CONSUMER

How to Win Your Personal Injury Claim, Matthews	1st Ed	$24.95	PICL
Nolo's Pocket Guide to California Law, Guerin & Nolo Press Editors	2nd Ed	$10.95	CLAW
Nolo's Pocket Guide to California Law on Disk	Windows	$24.95	CLWIN
	MAC	$24.95	CLM
Nolo's Law Form Kit: Hiring Child Care & Household Help, Repa & Goldoftas	1st Ed	$14.95	KCHLD
Nolo's Pocket Guide to Consumer Rights, Kaufman	2nd Ed	$12.95	CAG

IMMIGRATION

How to Get a Green Card: Legal Ways to Stay in the U.S.A., Lewis with Madlanscay	1st Ed	$22.95	GRN

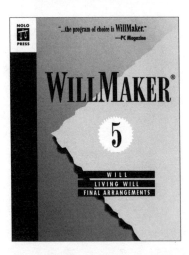

"...the program of choice is WillMaker."
—PC Magazine

WILLMAKER®

5

WILL
LIVING WILL
FINAL ARRANGEMENTS

SOFTWARE

WillMaker 5.0	Windows	$69.95	WI5
	DOS	$69.95	WI5
	MAC	$69.95	WM5
Nolo's Personal RecordKeeper 3.0	DOS	$49.95	FRI3
	MAC	$49.95	FRM3
Nolo's Living Trust 1.0	MAC	$79.95	LTM1
Nolo's Partnership Maker 1.0	DOS	$129.95	PAGI1
California Incorporator 1.0	DOS	$129.00	INCI
Patent It Yourself 1.0	Windows	$229.95	PYW1

LEGAL REFORM

Fed Up With the Legal System: What's Wrong and How to Fix It, Nolo Press	2nd Ed	$9.95	LEG

more books from Nolo Press

VISIT OUR STORE

If you live in the Bay Area, be sure to visit the Nolo Press
Bookstore on the corner of 9th & Parker Streets in west Berkeley.
You'll find our complete line of books and software—all at a
discount. CALL 1-510-704-2248 for hours.

ORDER FORM

CODE	QUANTITY	TITLE	UNIT PRICE	TOTAL

Subtotal	
California residents add Sales Tax	
Shipping & Handling ($4 for 1st item; $1 each additional)	
2nd day UPS (additional $5; $8 in Alaska and Hawaii)	
TOTAL	

Name

Address

(UPS to street address, Priority Mail to P.O. boxes)

FOR FASTER SERVICE, USE YOUR CREDIT CARD & OUR TOLL-FREE NUMBERS

Monday-Friday, 7 a.m. to 6 p.m. Pacific Time

Order Line	1 (800) 992-6656 (in the 510 area code, call 549-1976)
General Information	1 (510) 549-1976
Fax your order	1 (800) 645-0895 (in the 510 area code, call 548-5902)

METHOD OF PAYMENT

☐ Check enclosed

☐ VISA ☐ MasterCard ☐ Discover Card ☐ American Express

Account #   Expiration Date

Authorizing Signature

Daytime Phone

Allow 2-3 weeks for delivery. Prices subject to change.

NOLO PRESS, 950 PARKER ST., BERKELEY, CA 94710